Cedar Style

A Look at Lovely Log Homes

Roger Wade & Tina Skinner

Schiffer Publishing Ltd®

4880 Lower Valley Road Atglen, Pennsylvania 19310

Schiffer Books are available at special discounts for bulk purchases for sales promotions or premiums. Special editions, including personalized covers, corporate imprints, and excerpts can be created in large quantities for special needs. For more information contact the publisher:

Published by Schiffer Publishing Ltd.
4880 Lower Valley Road
Atglen, PA 19310
Phone: (610) 593-1777; Fax: (610) 593-2002
E-mail: Info@schifferbooks.com

For the largest selection of fine reference books on this and related subjects, please visit our web site at
www.schifferbooks.com
We are always looking for people to write books on new and related subjects. If you have an idea for a book please contact us at the above address.

This book may be purchased from the publisher.
Include $3.95 for shipping.
Please try your bookstore first.
You may write for a free catalog.

In Europe, Schiffer books are distributed by
Bushwood Books
6 Marksbury Ave.
Kew Gardens
Surrey TW9 4JF England
Phone: 44 (0) 20 8392-8585; Fax: 44 (0) 20 8392-9876
E-mail: info@bushwoodbooks.co.uk
Website: www.bushwoodbooks.co.uk
Free postage in the U.K., Europe; air mail at cost.

Library of Congress Control Number: 2007943477

Type set in Garamond

ISBN: 978-0-7643-2951-7
Printed in China

Acknowledgements

To Lani Laporte for her work in coordinating this entire project.

To Laura Mikowychok, for her work as copyeditor and writer. To Ginger Doyle for hours of adjustments. To Steve Biggs, Chairman of Town & Country Cedar Homes, and Allen Halcomb, President of MossCreek Designs, for their green light.

The following companies participated in this book, and stand at your beck and call to design and deliver custom made homes that rival the masterpieces featured here:

Town & Country Cedar Homes
800-968-3178
www.cedarhomes.com

MossCreek Designs
800-737-2166
www.mosscreek.net

Foreword

With an enduring enthusiasm for the beauty of natural wood homes that spans more than sixty years, the craftsmen of Town & Country Cedar Homes have fashioned award-winning log, timber, cottage and craftsman style using only the heart of Northern White Cedar. Cedar – a gift from Mother Nature - gives the home occupants an unparalleled living experience!

Town & Country Cedar Homes professionally manages the total turnkey building process, allowing the full enjoyment of first imagining, and then actually creating, one of the finest wooden homes in America – your own home! Prized by wood artisans, the inner core of white cedar is viewed as the most exquisite and durable of natural woods. With keen consideration for the environment, we harvest our cedar from the forests of Northern Michigan and Canada. Northern White Cedar is distinguished by a unique cellular structure that makes it resistant to rot, insects, and decay. It has consistent light coloring and, much like a cork, will not absorb moisture. Our kiln-drying process ensures a first quality product, which is then hand-hewn in our sawmill to exact design specifications, and engineered for the stability and longevity you desire in your home. Our commanding wall and roof systems are built 'green', providing a majestic home without sacrificing warmth, coziness and energy efficiency. With imagination and perfection, Town & Country builds one-of-a-kind homes as unique as the families who live in them.

Peruse the pages of this book to find seductively beautiful homes, designed with creativity and handcrafted with a commitment to perfection not found elsewhere in the industry. Work directly with the Town & Country's design team, now proudly associated with MossCreek, premier designers of custom mountain homes. HOME by MossCreek Designs embody the essence of mountain home style in genres such as Adirondack, Montana Big Sky and North Carolina Mountain themes.

Breathe in the essence of the finest wooden homes in America – a Town & Country Cedar Home! When you're ready to build the home you've always deserved to live in, we'll be here to provide you with complete personal support from our team of experienced Design Managers, at a Regional Design Center near you. Please call 800.968.3178 or visit us online at www.cedarhomes.com.

Stephen Biggs, Chairman
Town & Country Cedar Homes

Contents

Introduction

A home crafted from sturdy cedar timbers and tumbled fieldstone is ageless. Such structures as these date back to the Middle Ages, and record an achievement in craftsmanship that has varied little with the passage of centuries. Today's structures continue that heritage, enhanced by plate glass windows that seamlessly fuse the structure with its surroundings, and seal in comforts like HVAC, plumbing and state of the art appliances that update this timeless lifestyle.

An investment in a custom log or timber frame home, however, is more than money and futures. It's an opportunity to express oneself in a solid evidence of taste, be it a love of the wide open spaces of the Wild West and the Native American aesthetic, or an immersion in the storybook fantasy of stone and wood cottage dating back to the rural hillsides of Northern Europe. The luxury of a great room, soaring two stories to a cathedral ceiling, underscored in a massive stone hearth and wide-plank flooring is an investment in a very precious commodity – a space where one's imagination can take wing. Where a family can come together in a place where memories resonate amidst the warm aroma of baked goods from the kitchen, gentle strains of laughter, and the crackle of a warming fire.

Rock Solid

Who says rocks can't be warm and cozy? For this couple, indoor inspiration came from their front yard, where the goal was flawless landscaping with minimal upkeep, for plenty of charm minus the weeding, mowing, and edging. The answer was a rock-solid garden – literally! Paved with varying textures of loose gravel and small stones, and lined with beautiful boulders discovered during construction, this rock garden features flowers, trees, and a man-made stream flowing 360 degrees around the home. Inside, the landscaping was echoed in flag and river stone details like fireplaces, floors, pillars, and walls, for an interior that really rocks.

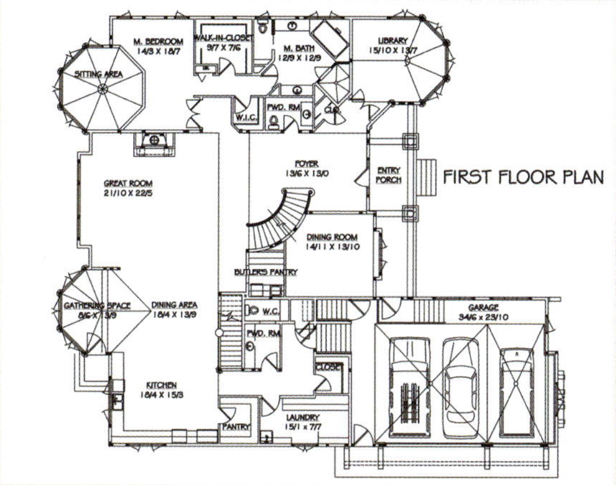

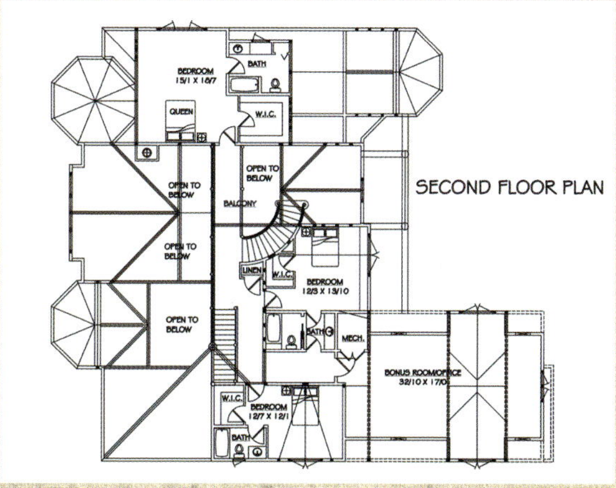

As a rock path approaches the home, the entrance is marked by two river stone pillars topped with trunks that support a grand, peaked roof cover. A unique half-round stone step leads to the porch, which features a brick back wall and a rock ledge that trims the door and several lower window edges.

In the evening, the stones reflect a blue shade similar to the sky, as paths of gathered stone snake around with the serpentine stream. Bright magenta flowers speckle the gardens mulched with stone.

In back, the stream gurgles past the many porches and sitting areas where the couple entertains and relaxes. The back wall is made of brick with cedar shake accents, and the twin radial bays are trimmed with hand hewn white cedar and flanked with a river stone wainscot.

At right, a pergola of logs that match the house's many posts and window panes stands tall to partially shade an outdoor dining space.

As one follows the stream through the front yard, benches beckon with their own unique views where one can stop and sit a while amidst the gardens, providing secret retreats that quickly become treasured relaxation spots. Note the tumbled rocks, "washed ashore" boulders, stream inlets and accidental water routes – when it comes to rock landscaping, it doesn't get any more natural-looking than this.

In the foyer of this home and throughout, no stone was left unturned. On the staircase, hand-forged wrought iron balusters climb the stairs; hand-hewn logs line the door frame; a vaulted ceiling of half-round logs peaks above the doorway like a cathedral; a square flagstone floor ties together the hues of tan, green, deep brown, and blue.

In the great room, stone takes center stage as it forms the raised hearth and climbing fireplace that runs floor to ceiling. A slab of deep-gray slate forms a hearth, and a natural log forms a sturdy mantle. Half-log paneling forms the northern white cedar walls of this room, and observe the tongue-and-groove paneling that flows stream-like down the back of the grand staircase.

This home's state-of-the-art kitchen features a river stone vent rising above the range top, and twin islands with granite tops provide a breakfast bar, prep area, and vegetable sink. Antique white cabinets with large trims and a vaulted ceiling above dominate this kitchen. Next door, an informal dining area is defined by a subtle oriental rug over the continous flagstone, and a radial bay gathering space provides a comfortablr spot where guests can linger over coffee or take in the aromas from the gourmet kitchen.

Viewed from the home theater lounge, a decorative, wood trimmed arched doorway leads gracefully to the lower level gathering space, where a flat-panel TV screen is mounted on a custom stone hearth. The bistro style bar and fully functional kitchen and billiard room beyond spell easy entertaining.

In the master bath, this couple enjoys a soaking tub surrounded by antique white bead board cabinets, with a slate-gray granite tub deck that matches their sink countertop. In the mirror, the glass doors of a tiled shower stall are visible.

A first-floor master bedroom lends a perfect view of the expertly landscaped back yard. A half-round outcropping holds a smart pick: a rounded sofa, which tucks neatly under the radial log ceiling to form a cozy, naturally lit lounge.

In this child's bedroom, a western-style canopy bed is complemented by an Indian blanket and other wild-west décor. A private bath adjoins this room. End matched paneling and log trim add further function to the gabled ceiling of this conventionally drywalled room.

Going Green

The seamless connection of open, functional indoor spaces with a dense surrounding forest is the great achievement of this suburban property. Tucked into a hidden gem of undeveloped, wooded sanctuary, the log home appears to have grown with the trees, and visitors pulling up the driveway believe they've stumbled upon a secret retreat. Inside, each window seems filled with a green wallpaper of sun and leaf; exposed beams trace the ceiling and walls, supporting the theory that the home simply grew to be. Outside, long porches encourage outdoor evenings; vast backyard expanses beckon touch-football teams, and the wall of trees beyond encloses the home inside a private, glowing-green fortress. Trees and shrubs tucked into the many corners of this home's exterior footprint prove that landscaping and log homes go hand-in-hand.

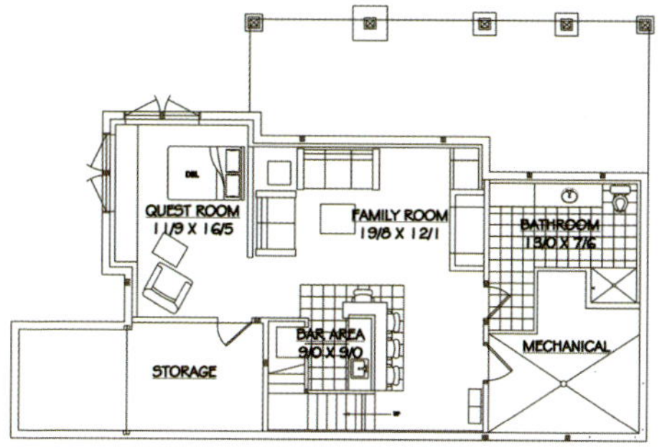

LOWER LEVEL PLAN

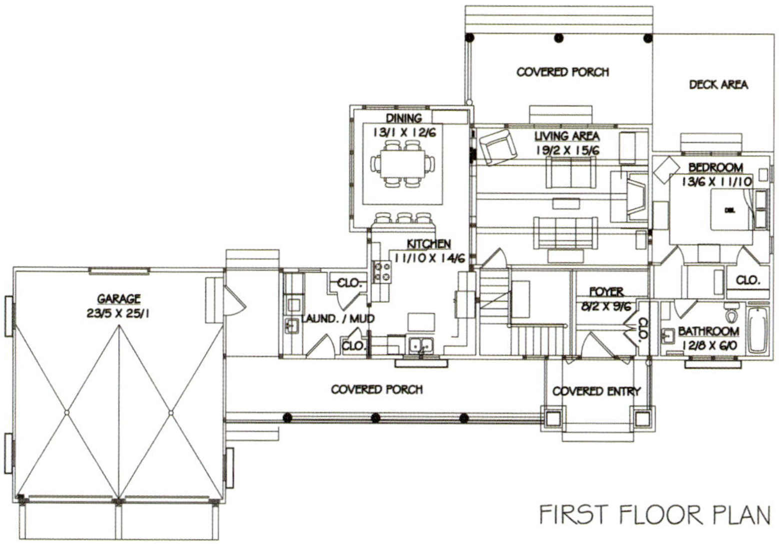

FIRST FLOOR PLAN

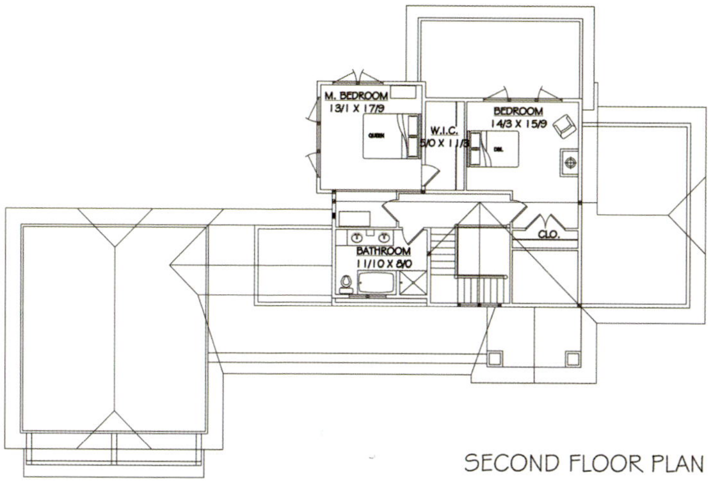

SECOND FLOOR PLAN

The front entrance to the home appears in the woods like a gateway to a hidden world. Stone pillars give a sense of permanence and strength, but lighter stones arranged organically give often-formal pillars a cozy lodge feel. From the front door, one can see straight through the home to the light and trees beyond.

Outside, no exterior face finds itself without large windows, sliding-glass doors, or relaxation-ready porches. The home's mild green color deepened by natural shade creates a calm and camouflaged exterior, and brown cedar shingle accents echo the colors of trees.

Inside, double sliding-glass doors and white cedar half log create an exterior wall, but never cut off the living room from the covered porch and the forest beyond. Recessed lighting is subtle, while highlighting the never-subtle drama of an exposed-log ceiling rafters. Interior walls painted green and trimmed in hand hewn wood echo the wall of trees at the lawn's perimeter.

A side-view of the back porch and deck reveals its smart anticipation of all kinds of weather: half is exposed to the sun and breeze, while the other half is ready to protect lovers of light rain showers, or create a cool refuge from summer heat. A gradual transition from in- to outdoors keeps the home feeling connected to nature, and porch-dwellers have a great view of wildlife, woods, and backyard games, for which there is plenty of open space.

The fire's glow is reflected in the northern white cedar ceiling, while the custom fieldstone fireplace adds the finishing touch to this Old English style log cottage.

The focal point of the living room, this fireplace of river rock is stacked to the ceiling and punctuated by a wooden log mantle. Placed with just enough order to be neat, the result resembles an exposed section of mountain.

The kitchen space, with its green-filled window, has a highly functional bar counter and layout, but preserves an aesthetic priority with buttercream cabinets complete with brushed nickel hardware and carved details, floral walls, and Tiffany-style café lighting.

The dining space is dressed in the outdoor green we've come to expect, but the motif is kept interesting with complementary red accents in unexpected places: mini lamp shades on the overhead light fixture, floral wallpaper, red seat cushions, and a thin, red rug trim.

In the master suite, picture-frame-like trim nicely surrounds windows that span almost the full height of the walls, and deep red drapery adds a textural contrast. Wood floors are warmed by area rugs in smart accent patterns, and a sleigh bed with red spread pops against canary walls. The bathroom repeats the wooden window trim, and features soft purple walls for added serenity.

This first-floor bedroom suite captures the greens and browns of the forest beyond. A familiar sliding glass door leads to the porch outside, while a recessed ceiling and cedar crown molding adds an unexpected architectural detail.

In this children's room, color and texture offer a youthful spin on sophisticated design. Block-paned windows give a storybook cottage look; an exposed wood floor is warmed by a child's rug, and bunk beds retain an unpainted finish to help wood details like hand hewn window trim and crown molding stand out.

In the Meadow

This cathedral-style timber beauty rises amidst the high grasses of a vast, flat meadow. Replete with skyward angles, clean lines, and perched atop river rock columns, the timberframe structure was clad in plank log siding accomplishing a contemporary, open style akin to beachfront vacation homes, but nestled in the meadows this family calls home. What results is an everyday dream vacation.

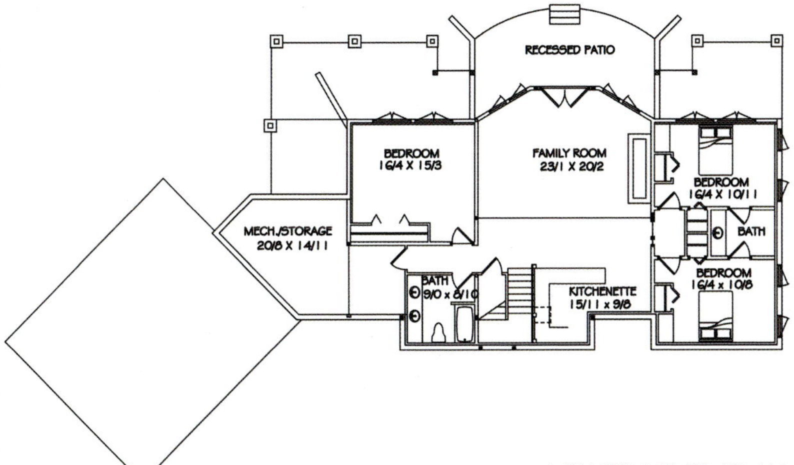

LOWER LEVEL PLAN

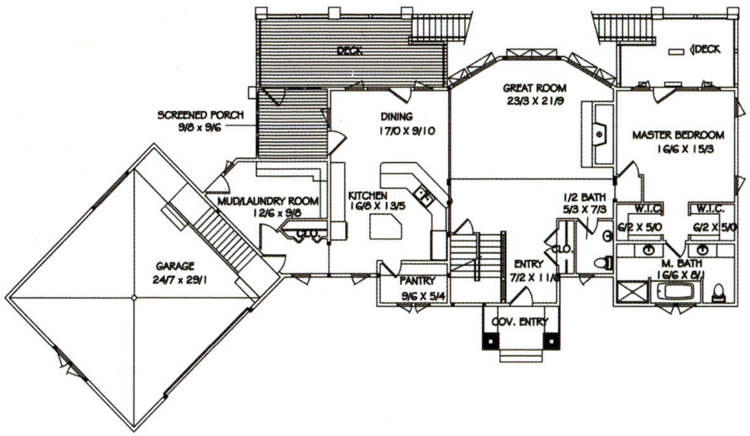

FIRST FLOOR PLAN

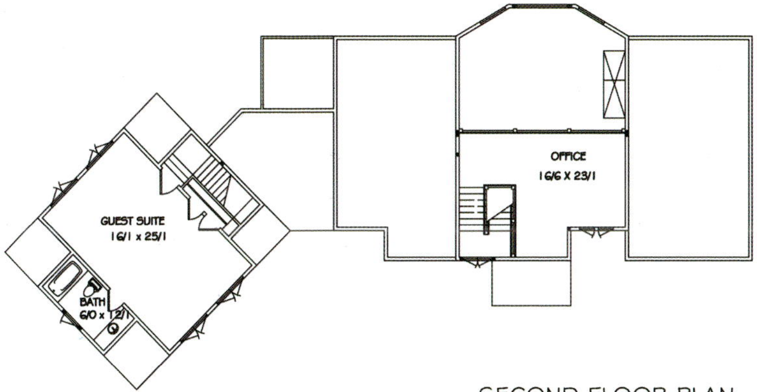

SECOND FLOOR PLAN

The front entrance, framed by stone pillars and wooden expressions of line and form, is punctuated by stylish lantern lighting.

Smartly, this home was situated with partial shade from one of the few trees on this open space, but the large windows were left entirely exposed, maximizing sunlight.

From the front, the structure appears to be a simple, single-level ranch home, and while a back walk-out is not a new idea, this home takes the concept to an entirely new level.

A cozy loft overlooks the open living room, and high among the handcrafted hammer trusses echoes the architectural timber peg features found at the main rear window, and the front door.

Once inside, lights and darks are married beautifully. Dark timber peg beams, sofas, and accents lie against light plaster-finished walls, pale river stones, and balusters. Lighting is a stand-out, with recessed, hanging, and track lighting all contributing to the drama of the dark beam work set against the contrasting white cedar tongue and groove cathedrial ceiling. A set of double love seats provides a great spot to take it all in.

The view from the dining space is spectacular of the expansive outdoor meadow, and of the vaulted cedar ceilings and impressive fireplace that seem to reach to the sky.

In the kitchen, stainless steel appliances, a geometric counter, island, ceiling angles, and recessed lighting transport you to an ultra-sleek designer kitchen showroom, while a stone archway, rustic tile floor, and plenty of exposed wood remind you that you're still in a cozy, yet custom home.

The master bedroom continues to juxtapose lights and darks, naturally light cedar trim creates a frame around each window's picturesque view, while dark curtains promise to darken the room for sleeping. An outdoor porch beckons beyond the textural drapery.

Rustic tile in the master bath is warmed by sandy wall tones and soft hand hewn wooden window trim.

Unexpected Surprise

It would be easy to approach this ranch style home with three-car garage façade and assume we know everything there is to know about its design. Step inside, and find exquisite details, unexpected interpretations, and high functionality; step around the back, and what emerges from the hillside is a striking display of angles, levels, and porches, for a house that truly celebrates the natural beauty of wood.

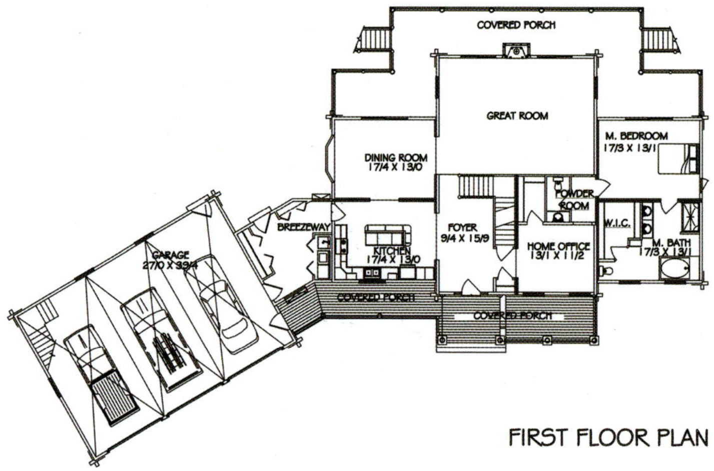

FIRST FLOOR PLAN

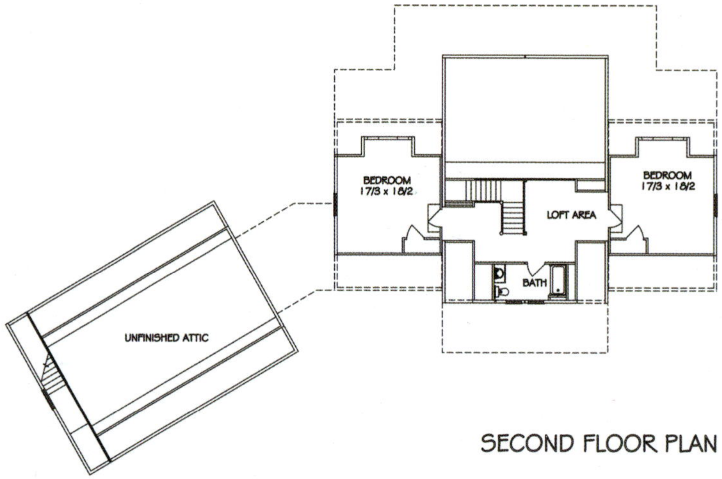

SECOND FLOOR PLAN

A wooden path previews the multitude of ways that wood creates texture, color, visual interest, and drama in this home. Complete with an arts-and-crafts-style lantern and a welcoming woodchuck who seems to be saying, "Look what I built!", is punctuated by full-round logs extending from a support wall within.

While only a teaser for what is to be found around the back of the house, this front porch showcases well the simple beauty of log and timber design – and warmly welcomes visitors, the task with which every porch is charged. The family's smiling Golden Labrador certainly doesn't hurt, either.

The rear porches speak for themselves. Massive cedar posts supporting log purlins and rafters are completed with white cedar beadboard ceilings. They have exquisite beauty, ample size and dramatic expanse, and though large enough for a sizable outdoor party, they remain personal and inviting.

Here, the foyer sets the stage for this wood-inspired house, with walls entirely of exposed log; the idea is continued with aplomb, preserving a natural ambience wherever you roam.

With logs forming every wall surface, this great room is a testament to log construction. A fireplace takes center stage on the far wall; a wide sitting area is filled with rich leather furniture and defined by an Oriental rug. On the far side, an intimate sitting area is created by cozy, oversized reading chairs, angled to each other.

On the interior wall of the great room, a natural hewn, northern white cedar staircase rail winds upward.

Not to be outdone, the kitchen finds ways to carry its weight in wooden themes. The cabinetry, counters, and stools embody the light tones of the other rooms' wooden walls; soft canary kitchen walls carried into the dining room unify the eating spaces, and a stone tile floor ties the different shades together.

A set of glass French doors opens into the bright dining room that takes advantage of a great view.

In the master bedroom, the porch is accessed by an extra-wide sliding glass door – a dramatic custom detail that adds to the expansive feel.

Down the hall, another bedroom features a unique dormer with bay window – the perfect spot to position two chairs for quiet conversation, book-reading, or taking in the spectacular view from the top floor.

The entire home features the natural beauty of wood; why should the bathroom be any different? Exposed wood graces the window trim, frames the double-bowl vanity mirror, serves as the cabinet doors and drawer faces – even encircles the soaking tub – giving what is traditionally a room of synthetic material a natural, warm appeal.

Welcome Home

This spectacular log home design calls to mind deep mountain lodges where hearths contain crackling fires, expansive views preview week-long vacations of skiing or hiking, and quiet corners offer the perfect place to curl up with a book. Truly a daily getaway, the home embodies everything a log or timber design should be: unexpected, dramatic, and custom at every corner.

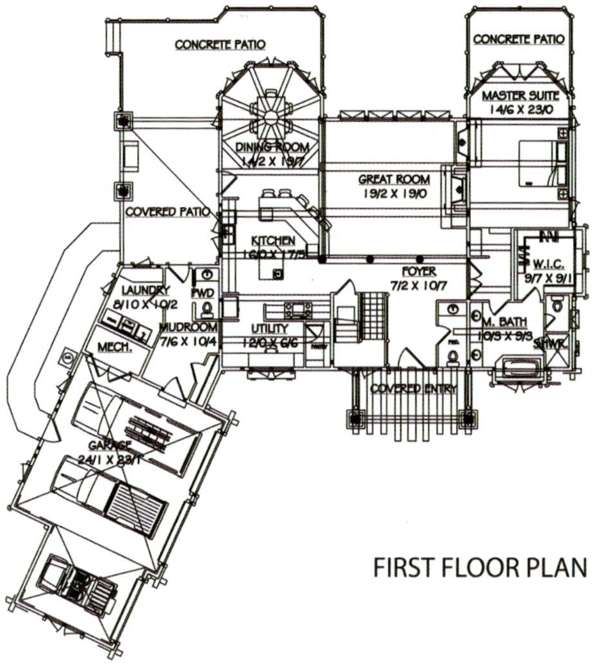

FIRST FLOOR PLAN

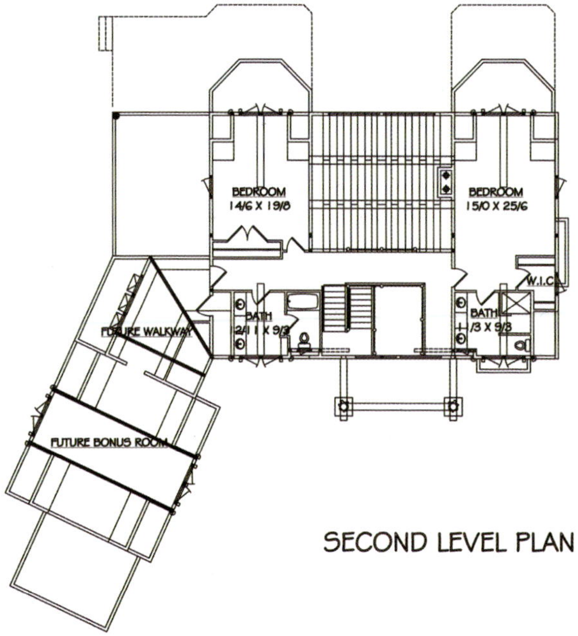

SECOND LEVEL PLAN

A modest profile previews a refined western motif that will permeate the house, and features a unique connected three-car garage where the owners have added a bonus room on the second level for space to expand.

The glass wall of the great room takes center stage, surrounded by extensive cedar decking with room to roam over the plains.

An evening view reveals magical lighting choices, creating a warmth that beckons visitors inside or explores the entertainment options in the covered outdoor kitchen and sitting area.

A spectacular great room awaits inside, featuring floor-to-ceiling windows, a towering stone fireplace with natural log mantle, and larger-than-life king trusses that cross the room. Antiques and cowhide carry the western atmosphere to new heights.

When the natural light dims, a wrought-iron chandelier tucked into the trusses provides an evening glow over the great room sitting area, where double love seats provide the perfect gathering place.

A catwalk passes over the great room, offering a closer view of the wood paneling and the peak of the windows that rise to the height of the cathedral ceilings. Hand-hewn log railings create a sturdy, woodsy path from room to room.

A wagon wheel hub crowns the radial dining area. A side view shows how seamlessly the foyer and dining areas are connected, separated only by a bar service counter framed by uniquely hewn cabinetry.

In upstairs bedrooms, sloped ceiling planes are broken up by tall dormers that hold cozy window seats. An oversized wooden headboard helps to size the bed to the height of the room, while a cowboy boot lamp, tin star wall art, and studded leather rocker set a western mood. Tongue and groove ceilings showcase the dramatic ceiling lines.

A rock island continues the mountain outcropping tones into the kitchen while partitioning the two rooms. Dinnerware and accents in reds and blues break up the browns, tans, and grays of this kitchen's exposed beams, custom cabinetry, and steel appliances. A stone surround enfolds a stainless steel cooking center.

The master bedroom is a showcase of light and beams, influenced by the great room of which the builders were so proud. A stone fireplace with wooden mantle repeats in this room, as do the ceiling beams, and a bear lamp helps to forest the scene.

Logs insulate an outside wall of the master bath, where a soaking tub trimmed with earthy tile waits beside a shower with a mountaintop etched glass door. Natural light beams in the two tub-side windows, but when the shades are drawn, soft recessed lighting steps in.

A vanity is divided by deep shelving, and delicate bulb lanterns illuminate a double-bowl sink of marble.

Oh, the Triumphs of Trees

Only in fairytales are homes built of trees, their branches and roots forming woven walls and winding staircases. But inside this very real lakeside property, trees seem to have performed the role of architect, contractor, and interior designer. Step inside for a home that feels like you never left the forest.

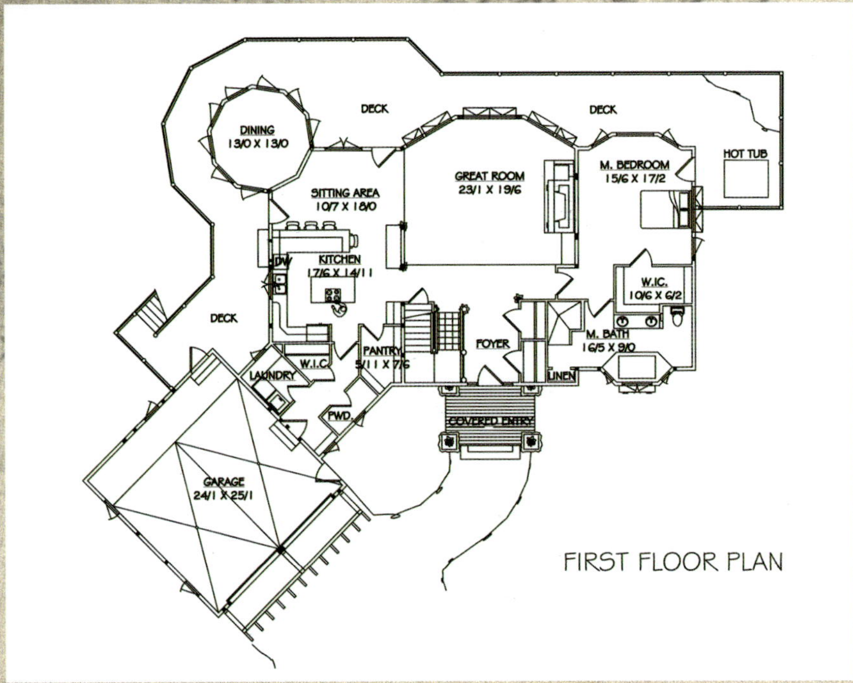

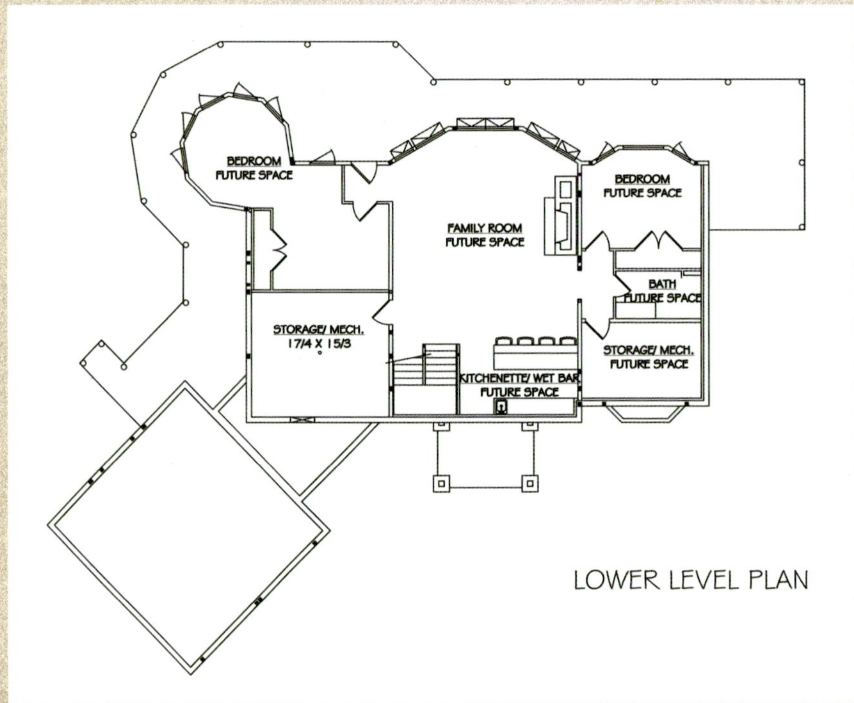

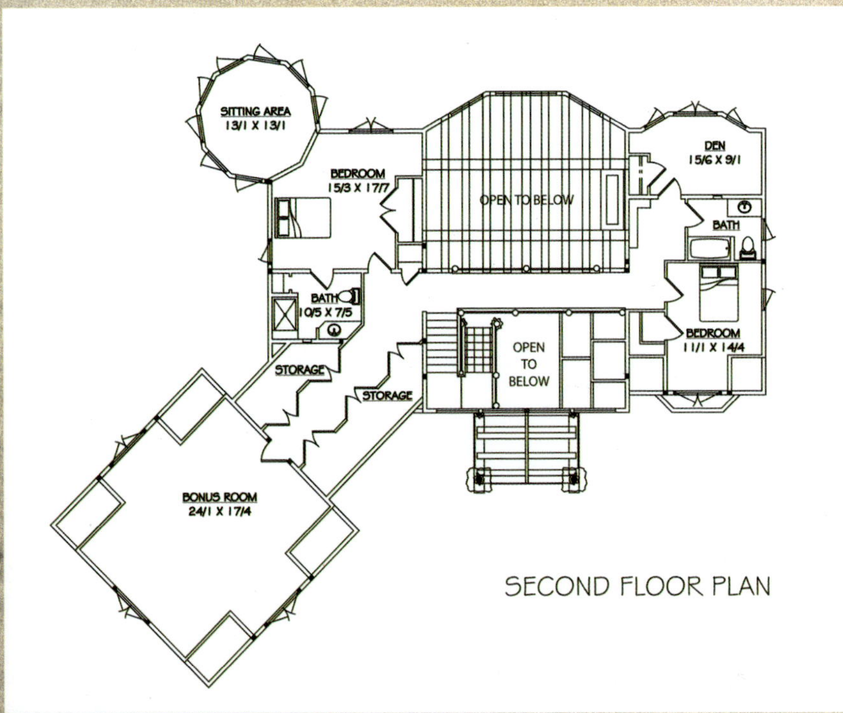

Interesting angles and architectural detail make the front of this home a fascinating journey for the eyes. Scanning the façade, riverstone surfaces contrast with bright brown wood finishes, a custom door with a uniquely curved frame creates a focal point, and finished trees with hand hewn flare bases support a portico protecting the entrance.

Windows ensure the owners can enjoy spectacular views of the lake below from almost every room, on every level.

A sandy beach and lots of chairs allow bathers to rest while waiting for a boat ride.

A peak of windows and angled beams creates a cliff top effect that resembles the very ledge on which this house sits. A wide porch creates ample space for outdoor gathering.

Tall posts suspend the back porches over a dramatic slope and serpentine stone path to the lake.

A fire crackles in a towering great room fireplace of uneven river rock, and a curved sofa of deep brown leather invites fireside conversations. From here, one can take in the grandeur of a floor-to-ceiling window.

An earthy tile floor connects the many hues of wood and stone in the great room and foyer. The staircase and in-room posts remember their roots, flaring slightly like the natural tree itself. Scattered knots create a textural wall pattern, making this wood paneling the easiest wallpaper decorators have ever applied.

The main level's open layout helps the eye transition easily between rooms and around the many custom details. Wagon-wheel frames of king post trusses soar overhead.

Following an indoor tree-lined path into the kitchen, one finds knotty cabinetry against plaster-finished walls, reflective granite countertops, and a stone tile floor that ties each hue to a common canvas. Two flared cedar posts enfold a granite topped serving counter, doubling as a convenient seperation between food preparation and great room areas.

Not one, but two dining spaces furnished with hand-hewn log chairs create a welcome spot to break bread with friends. Overhead, a wagon-wheel beam hub traces the structure of the octagonal room.

Over the dining room and connected to the upstairs bedroom, a home office capitalizes on the windows that encircle this corner of the house. In this inspiring room, the working executive can be at his or her most creative, under a radial bay dome of northern white cedar.

A catwalk open to the great room below provides an impressive close-up of the sophisticated ceiling angles and wood joinery, and offers hidden spots for storage and décor, such as this family's upstairs library. A rustic cabin-style chandelier hangs at eye-level on the catwalk.

In the bathroom, a deep soaking tub is encased in earthy tile. Light blinds provide privacy from other porch views, but always let in the sun.

The master bedroom and bath feature exquisite views through unique window arrangements. Cedar paneled ceilings help reflect light, and a bed constructed of the same wood unites the room. Access to the extensive outdoor decking creates an opportunity for viewing starlit nights!

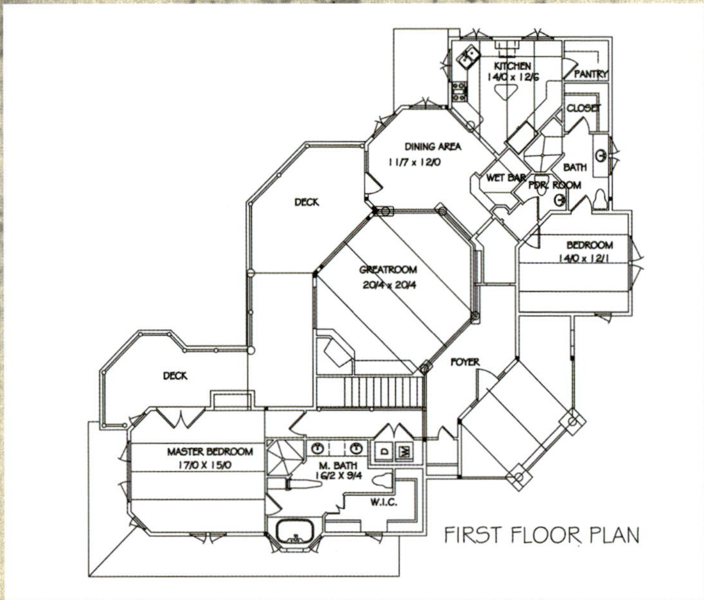

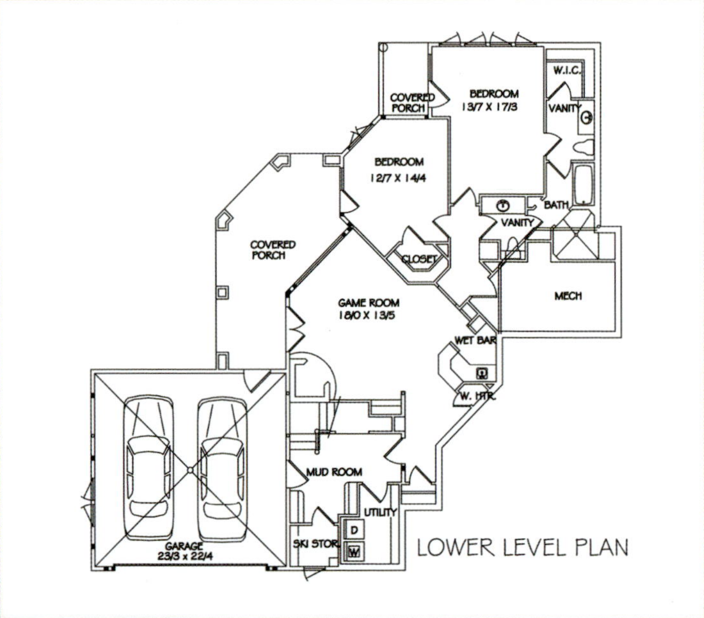

Mountain Majesty

A family's love for entertaining guided the design for this vacation abode nestled in the mountains. With open space for gathering, dining, gaming, listening to music, and more, the home achieves a great balance: roomy spaces ready to party, and cozy corners where day-afters can be spent with a good book. For this family, it is a vacation home destined to be shared with friends.

With views like these, who could stay inside? Expansive wrap-around decks with unobtrusive iron railings extend over the rear slope, making for a majestic view of the mountains and forest. Sliding glass doors open the great and dining rooms directly out to the deck, creating a charming pass-through for large get-togethers during any season.

Camouflaged by the nature of its design, the rough hewn cedar timbered home is no stranger to the area's abundant deer, birds, and other natural wildlife. Windows afford anyone peeking out a moment of natural wonder with friendly mountain "neighbors."

With a chandelier of antlers overhead, a staircase of natural twig railing to the left, and an enormous great room of artifacts and architecture beyond an open pass-through, the mountain region and a forest ambience is previewed for all who enter the foyer.

In the great room, dramatic beams, a natural wood mantle, and wood trim around floor-to-ceiling windows bring close the trees outside, while hunting rifles, antler lamps, and tree stump end tables provide great cabin atmosphere.

The amateur chef is spared cabin fever in this enormous kitchen, complete with vast marble counters for prep work, a six-burner range, and an island for mobile working space. Early risers can slide up to a breakfast bar on a natural log stool and take in the beam work overhead while breakfast is prepared.

For more formal dining, a large wooden table waits in the dining room under another antler chandelier. Note the glass doors leading to the deck beyond, and the ever-present oversized windows that let in tons of natural light.

In a custom home built for entertaining, a stereo playing generic mingling music wouldn't be enough. Instead, guests can find a spot to pause with their glass of wine to listen or make requests at the family's baby grand piano – just another way they've customized the gathering experience. And with the acoustics of a home filled with vaulted ceilings, this vacation home quickly fills with music.

On the lower level, a custom bar and recreation area are filled with conversation-starters. This western-themed room is complete with rodeo artifacts, cowboy art, and Native American fabric patterns straight from saddle blankets.

In the master bedroom, a bed built by the forest sits beneath a cedar paneled ceiling and windows arranged to look like hung pictures. On a bed pillow, an embroidered blessing reads, "May the peace of the wilderness be with you."

In the master bath, the bathtub is creatively tucked into an unobtrusive bump-out beneath a bay window.

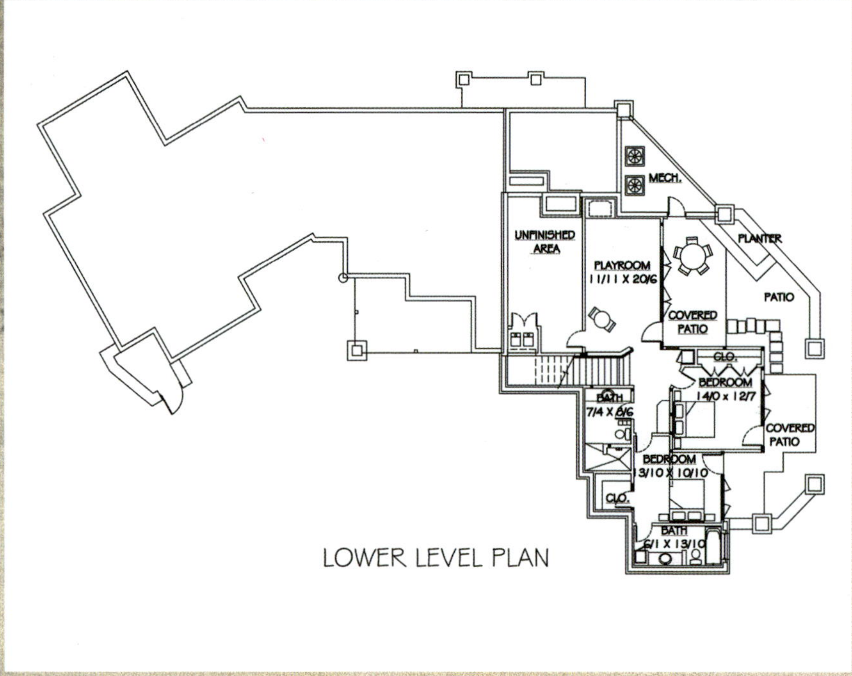

LOWER LEVEL PLAN

Beauty and the Beam

In a room filled with artifacts and art, why would anyone stare at the ceiling? Beams are the answer in this beautiful, contemporary home traced with massive, strong, and oh-so-dramatic timber framing. The artistic couple wanted a home as visually interesting as the art in their personal collections; so successful was the design, you might say their pieces have been upstaged. From the inside out, the structural elements of this house left the artists feeling right at home, and continue to leave their guests breathless.

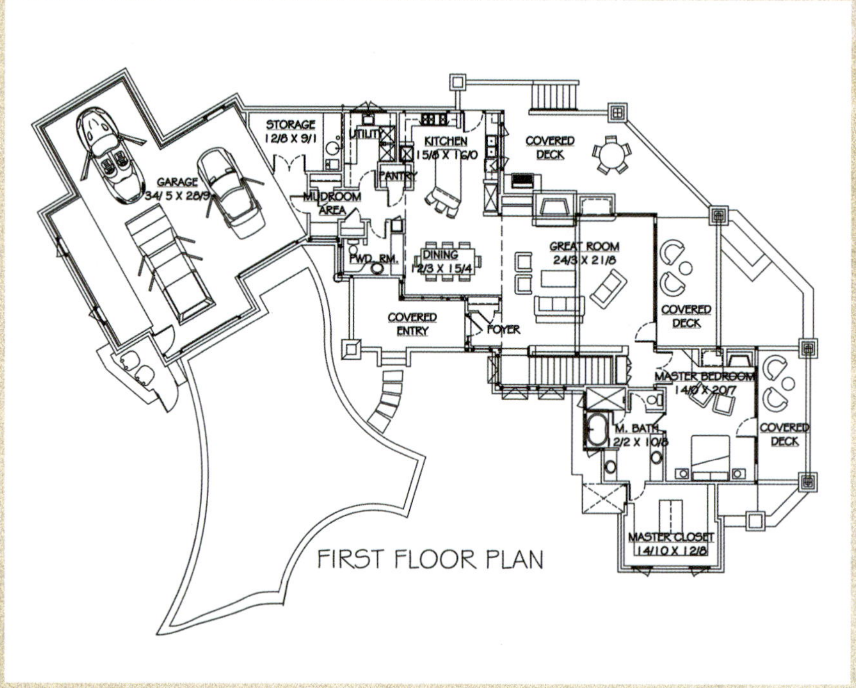

FIRST FLOOR PLAN

Timber trusses crowned by standing seam red metal roofing combine with durable rough cut timber siding and chinking to create the authentic style of a western mining cabin.

Light spills across the sheltered entryway and stone foyer warms the snow outside a cozy dining room.

The exposed chimney in the great room features country fieldstone, at once both organic and geometric, creating an angular yet accidental composition. The fireplace reaches from floor to ceiling, and features a mock-mantle that nicely grounds a centrally suspended still-life. A built-in bookshelf to the left holds this couple's many artifacts from travels abroad.

A contemporary off-white ledge at left conceals the staircase headed to the lower level. A bench for two completes the space.

(opposite)
The great room is a tribute to exposed beams. Set against creamy plaster-finished walls, the dark finish of these massive timbers is a perfect contrast to draw the eye up and over the peaked ceiling to take in the entire room. As the sun peers into this room, light is cast over the deep tones of the wooden floor, softened with an Oriental rug that ties together unique chair fabric, caramel leather sofas, and accents in shades of pink, brown, and butter yellow. In the evenings, spotlighting simulates sunlight streaming through the overhead trusswork.

An island performs triple-duty in this functional, beautiful kitchen. With drawer and cabinet storage below, workspace and veggie sink built into the top counter above, and a charming bar for informal dining at the far end, the island is an irreplaceable part of this kitchen. The exposed timbers continue into this room, making the kitchen as visually stunning as the great room.

The elegant tile backsplash of the custom range provides the hues of pink, copper, and deep gray found in each room, framed, of course, by rich wood.

The dining room features an enormous sunswept window with custom blinds, a chandelier of hammered wrought iron, and a stone tile floor that unites the many earth tones at work in this room.

For the couple's master bedroom, the woodwork is simplified to calm eye movement around the room and encourage rest. Clean lines of wood and a handful of recessed lights look down upon a headboard carved with branches, and finished with a bedspread of pretty pink and beige paisleys. Across the room, a simple hearth with tiled slate creates a peaceful visual, and glass panels form a luminous connection across the sitting area to the private deck.

Dark accents continue to create visual contrast in the master bath. Smart choices like dark colored faucet, deep brown towels and wooden venetian blinds do the job nicely.

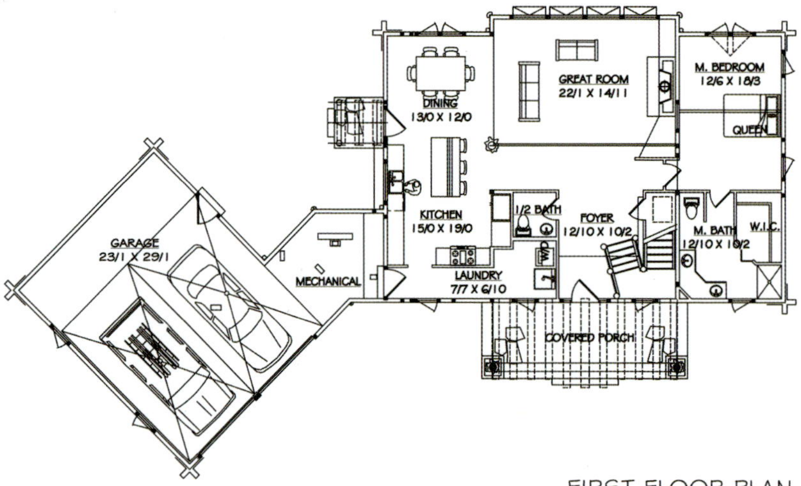

FIRST FLOOR PLAN

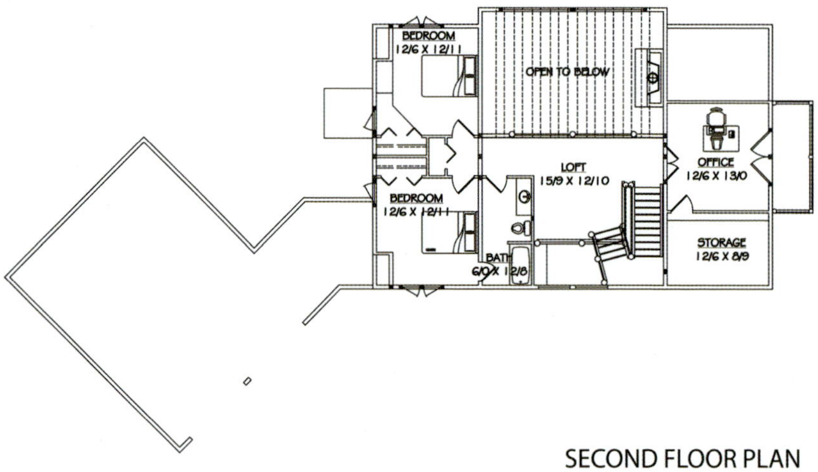

SECOND FLOOR PLAN

Nook and Cranny

This stand alone log home in the foothills is a marvel of compactness, pictured here on its wooded lot after a fresh snow. With high roofs of angles reaching skyward, the home builds up, rather than out, and utilizes hidden places as useful spaces. Natural log finishes construct the walls from the inside out, and custom details in wood and stone make this home truly luscious log home living on the western ftont.

Twin peaks form the interesting façade of the western style log home with textural surfaces of both cedar shingle and exposed beaming. Natural tree trunk shapes form the two entry pillars nicely as they stand upon two columns of tightly stacked ledgestone. A custom carved front door mimics exposed beams with an arrangement of solid wood and glass panes.

Around the back, more peaks of knobby log ends and triangular windows break up horizontal rooflines. Note the unique cutout design of the extreme top of each gable peak; mimicing the craggy outcroppings of the nearby nountains.

The great cutouts of the custom front door help keep the small foyer open and airy, while speckling the floor with fragmented light. Cedar paneling helps reflect sunlight throughout the space. A great stacked-log staircase rises on the left, featuring deep-cushioned wooden steps.

In the kitchen, cedar paneling continues to reflect light from every source – the large window over the sink, the café-style lighting over the island and breakfast bar, and the recessed lighting pocketed within the ceiling itself. Pastel green walls and a pale tile floor keep the light moving and set the room aglow. Custom details such as the range and counter backsplashes bring color and subtlety to every corner.

The beauty of the wild west is best viewed alongside the treasured heirlooms, rustic finishes, and distinctive hand hewn logs of a northern white cedar home.

The soft green kitchen tones are carried into the dining room, where blue and red accents provide unexpected bold color and a large window helps the smaller room feel open.

In the master bedroom, a high ceiling results in a space that feels as large as the great room. Pale lilac encourages a restful, quiet atmosphere and the cedar log wall and paneled ceiling compliment the coziness. A chair built for two sits under the room's two large windows, both with stunning views of the mountainside.

(opposite)
In the great room, the tight stacks of stone that form the entryway columns are echoed in the fireplace, around which charming tan wingback chairs and a unique plaid sofa are gathered. A floor-to-ceiling window rises to the roof peak. Never obstructing the view, elongated, space-saving wall sconces were tucked within the valuable real estate of log-trimmed window framework.

A multi-level countertop in marbled greens and yellows creates a stunning palette in the master bathroom.

Upstairs, a sitting area is tucked into the peak of a roof over the foyer, and what would normally be a quick catwalk between rooms is transformed into a livable space.

In the upstairs bedroom, walls of exposed log and ceilings of matching cedar paneling are broken up by choice accents of blue. With amazing views, this room just had to include a pair of oversized windows.

Crafted by the Lake

A beautiful lake-front lot challenged both budget and aesthetics for a family that dreamed of having it all. Limiting themselves to a relatively small footprint, the homeowners wanted a structure that would rise up to encompass a lake view, while offering an architectural profile perfect for this wooded, wilderness retreat. Log was their adamant choice, but they also wanted more than a cabin. They wanted a soaring great room with windows expansive enough to catch the lake's reflected light and flood their living spaces. They wanted an architectural profile that challenged the Adirondack style associated with log homes in their region. Most importantly, though, they wanted a retreat home with exciting social spaces where they could congregate, and small retreat rooms where they could find solitude and the silence expected from a getaway.

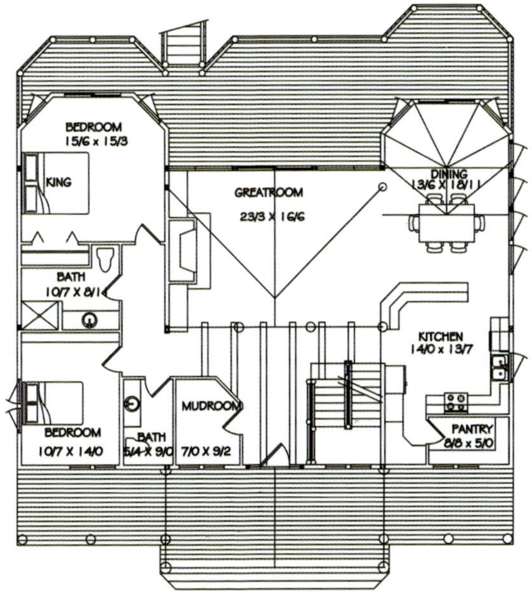

FIRST FLOOR PLAN

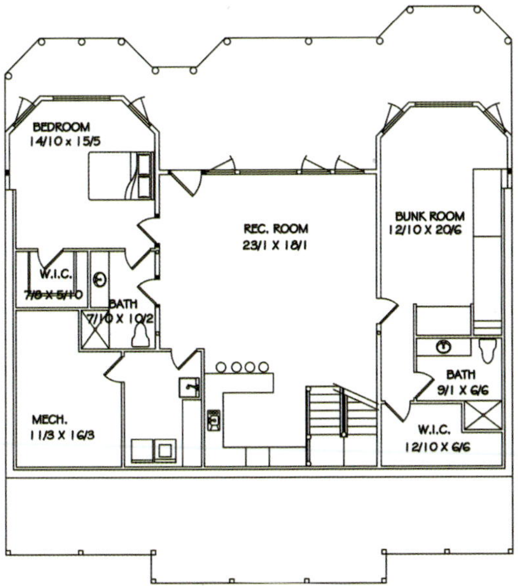

LOWER LEVEL PLAN

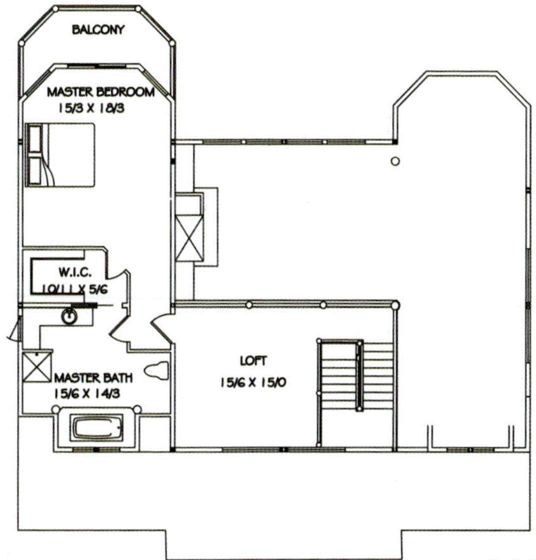

SECOND FLOOR PLAN

From first approach it's obvious this is no ordinary log home. An entry porch is crowned with a truss and purlin supported roof. A bridge provides an elevated approach.

A bear and window boxes characterize the hand-hewn lodge log style of this home, crafted with northern white cedar saddle notched corners.

A wooden bridge creates an architectural connection between this beautiful home and the lake beyond. A third-floor suite was added, tower-like, to command a view of the waters.

Deck and patio hug every angle of the home's lakeside view, creating endless gathering spaces and outdoor entertainment opportunities.

Carefully chosen furnishings establish a rustic American atmosphere, from Native American textiles to locally obtained hunting trophies. In fact, wildlife becomes a theme in the home, much as it is beyond, where the windows often provide the reward of glimpsed creatures just beyond the walls. Local river stone climbs both the chimney and tops the hood in the kitchen, adding natural counterpoint to the wood surroundings. Striking walls of tree length northern white cedar with chinking works its way up to a maze of log raftered angles on the ceiling.

A breathtaking view of blue waters is served with each meal in the dining room, where family members gather around a hand-crafted table for the fare. Also popular are the bar stools scooted close to the cook's kitchen, each backed by a woodland scene in wrought iron.

A quiet alcove keeps this rustic cabin connected to the world beyond, with internet access and the occasional chance to "work from home."

Custom hand crafted items, like the cedar sink base with branches make a one-of-a-kind statement in the powder room.

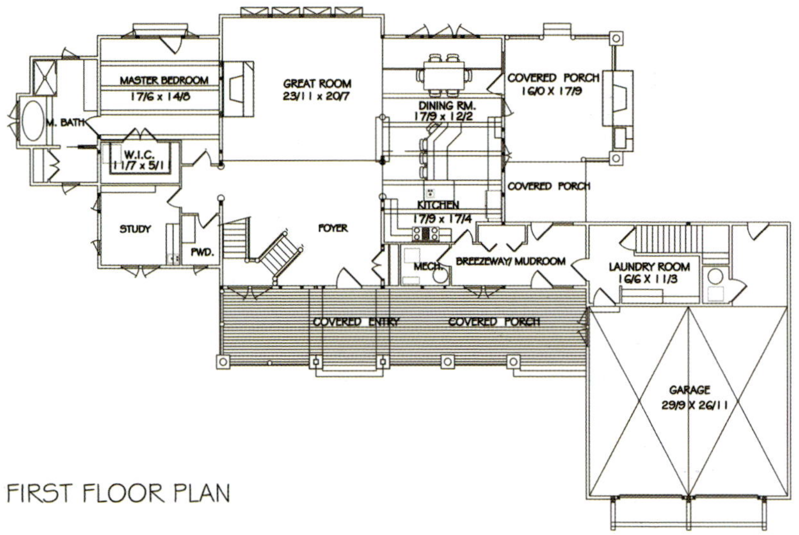

FIRST FLOOR PLAN

Uniquely Situated

In setting out to design a custom log home, this family wanted to make sure that they got just that – custom. A craftsman style sensibility, dating back to the aesthetics of the 1930s Arts and Crafts movement, was carefully incorporated into the architecture of their home, most notably in the partial-stone support columns that welcome visitors to the home, as well as the timber trimmed garage door that adds a special touch to the home's curb appeal. The craftsman look was carried throughout the interior of the home as well, with furnishings and handcrafted details. With all this attention to detail, a special place was also designed to provide a separate and yet connected space for a mother-in-law suite over the garage.

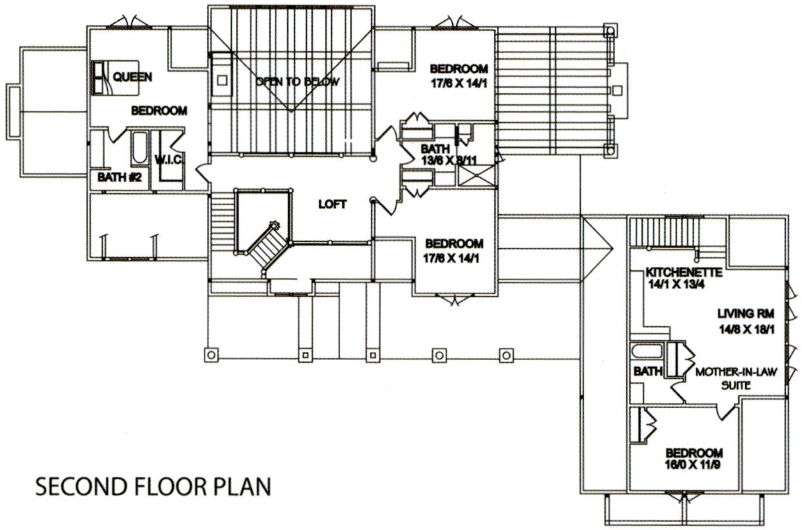

SECOND FLOOR PLAN

Extended cornices on the roofline, as well as dormers to help vary it, enhance the sense of character this home portrays. Tumbled pavers lend a sense of age in an artfully laid out drive and entry walk.

A stone retaining wall elevates the home and defines it within an expansive backyard play area.

Every aspect of the foyer announces this home as unique, from the slate flooring and on up the angled, flared post staircase. The owner's love of the Arts and Crafts Era is announced through lighting fixtures, and the visitor is on his or her way to a tour surely worth that fifty cents!

Massive structural log trusses define the cathedral ceiling above the family room. See-through cabinetry with slumped glass surrounds the bar area between living room and kitchen, affording easy access to libations.

An outdoor living and eating area is the pleasing alternative to indoors whenever weather permits family members to move closer to the lake-front view. This magnificent fireplace is certainly an inducement, even when it's chilly.

Blinds are raised high to leave the lake views unfettered in the dining room.

Rustic log beams, cedar walls and antique finishes create contrast in the kitchen area, where a raised counter invites family members to belly up while the cook prepares their treats.

A lofty nook invites, serving both as landing access to the three second-floor bedrooms, but also a quiet place to slip away during the day and hide with a good book.

A tile surround creates access to a sunken retreat in the master bath, complete with a private, wooded view.

A one-of-a-kind bed frame fits perfectly in this cedar lined bedroom and is the perfect ending to a house unique in every way.

Allarmingly Charming

A chalet appears, seemingly transported from another time, another continent. This storybook apparition appears like a treasure unveiled at the edge of a hilltop meadow. Timber frame architecture harks back to medieval craftsmanship, and a splash of stucco and revealed stone add awe to this utterly charming edifice. Don't be fooled by the fairy tale façade, though – the owners of this home enjoy spacious comforts, and magnanimous views across their secluded waterfront estate.

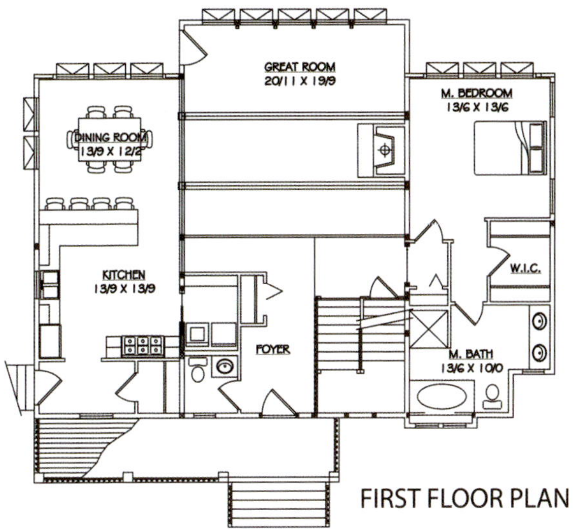

FIRST FLOOR PLAN

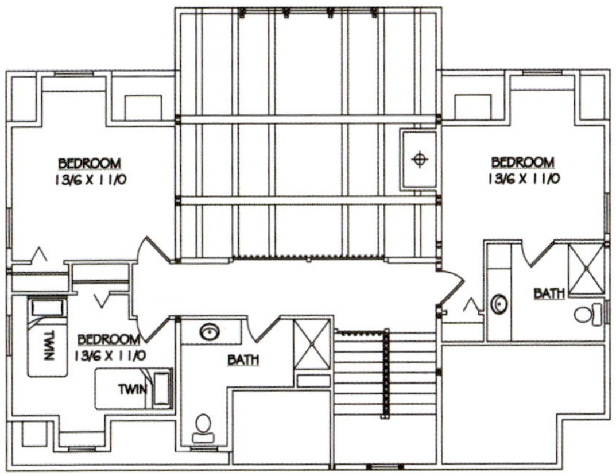

SECOND FLOOR PLAN

The combined uses of stone, different colors of wood, stucco, shingled roof, and varied styles of windows make this home very appealing to the eyes.

A different home in back, the architecture of the rear was built around a wall of window, with every room afforded a generous view of the naturally preserved waterfront setting.

Up close, the charm of intricate detail continues, from the custom gable accent trimmed with timber brackets, to the porthole window handsomely framed against cedar shingle siding.

Inside that wall of windows rises a cathedral ceiling, artfully supported by hammer-beam timbers that shelter the warm gathering places below. A study of light and dark, the cedar paneled ceiling was stained to match window and floor moldings, while leather furniture coordinates with the architectural supports for a pleasing two-tone effect.

The open floor plan created by massive timber frame support allows for a connectedness between the kitchen, dining, and living areas. The three areas were tied together through the use of a common wood finish for moldings and cabinetry.

This master suite also commands its own private bank of windows. Tile and stone create a nature-inspired surround for the soaking tub.

Tucked under eaves, a guest room creates a fortress-like feel for grandchildren, complete with private lookouts.

Part and Parcel

Seeming to have grown organically on the spot, this lakefront home was built in accord with its privileged place. Outside, natural boulders were allowed to form the landscape, and inside, real tree trunks were incorporated to support a structure designed in every way to maximize the experience of a lake getaway. Inside, botanical prints in art and textiles, living plants, and natural surfaces add to the connectedness one experiences throughout the landscape of this beautiful log home.

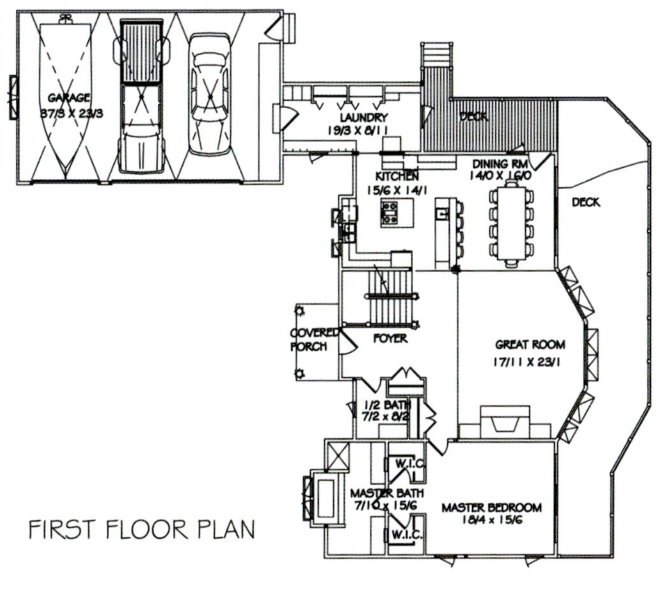

FIRST FLOOR PLAN

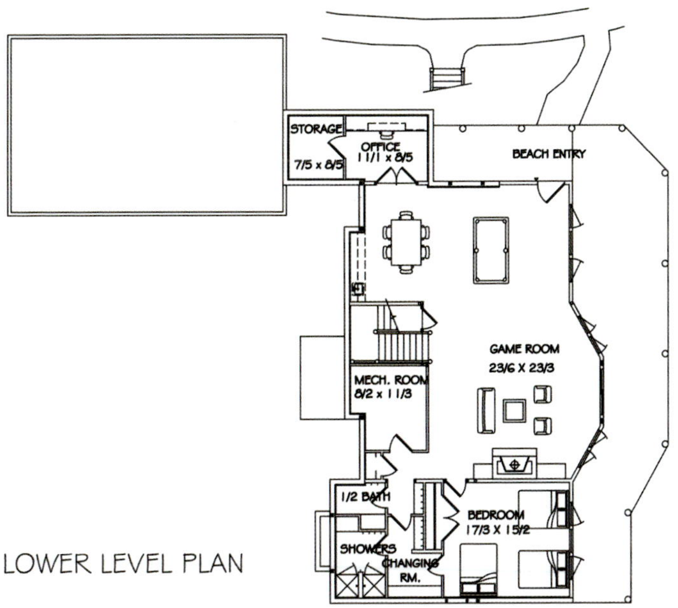

LOWER LEVEL PLAN

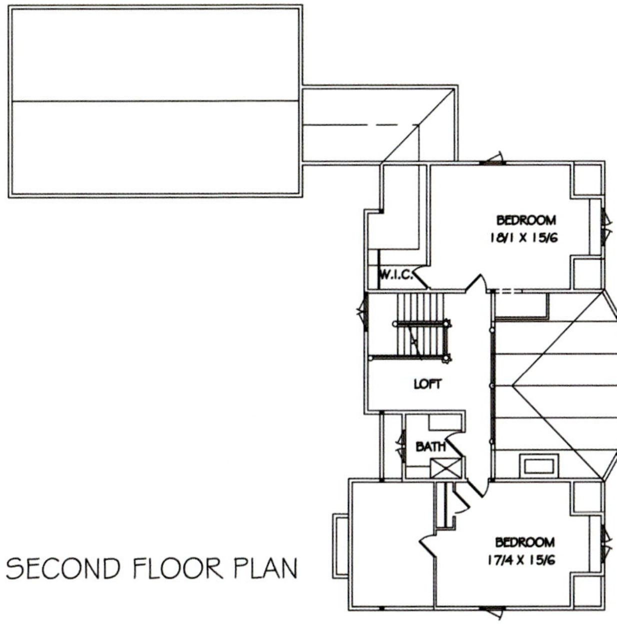

SECOND FLOOR PLAN

A pillared entryway provides an architectural invitation to a front porch that seems to rise from the stone boulders surrounding it. A pond on one side and a running stream on the other add the music and movement of water to this handsome approach.

Boulders surround a reflecting pond just off the back patio, where a lower level walkout opens a recreation room to the world. Above, a Plexiglas balustrade provides a safety barrier for the first-floor deck without obstructing the view.

Guests gather at a casual raised counter overlooking the kitchen during most gatherings. Cedar paneling helps conceal a state-of-the-art refrigerator in this artfully countrified gourmet kitchen.

(opposite and above)
A two-story great room forms the central gathering place for the home. For the visitor, it is an impressive first step off the foyer into the living area. Here red upholstery punctuates a conversational circle, set against an artfully framed glass view of the lake. A stone hearth and wrought iron chandelier suffuse the room with a warm glow.

The dining table is surrounded by comfortably stuffed chairs that encourage guests to linger and savor their meals. Sliding doors finesse the line between inside and out.

The fun gets serious on the lower level of the home, where a gaming area provides a variety of leisure activities at ground level.

A stone bowl was hollowed for an artful touch in a powder room.

Windows characterize the master suite, both above a whirlpool bath, and along two outside walls overlooking the lake.

A window seat tucks up to a view of the lake, sheltered behind the roofline and a fortress of four posters.

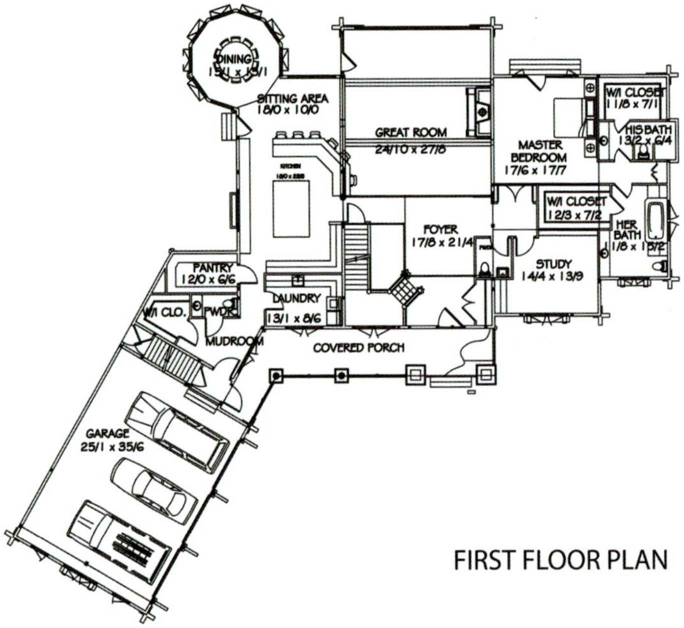

FIRST FLOOR PLAN

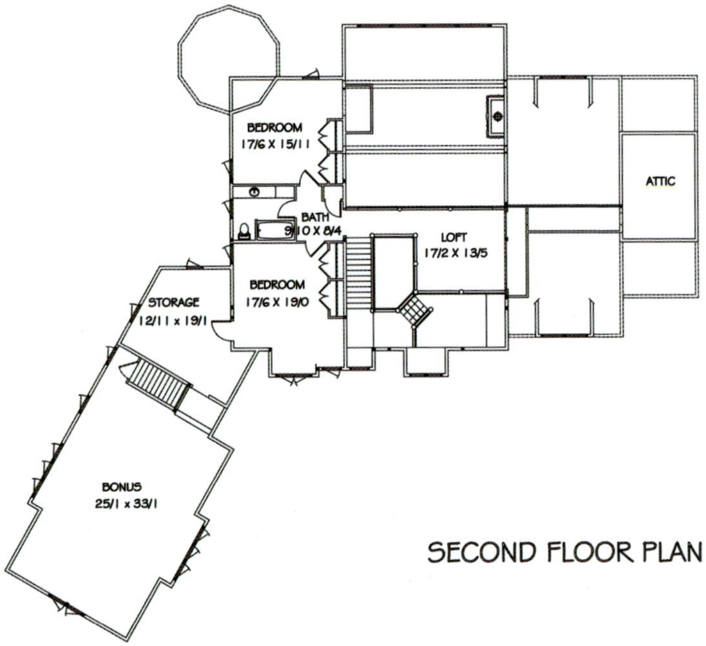

SECOND FLOOR PLAN

On Private Pond

A perfect setting required a house no less so. The owners helped design their home – part log, part timber frame – that is architecturally pleasing while custom fit to their living needs. Practicality ruled as they laid out a series of rooms that progressed logically, from a family garage entrance that passed through the mudroom and laundry, to the pantry and kitchen. The home expands through a great room, and on to a master suite complete with his and her bathrooms. Guests enter through an impressive foyer, while bedrooms adjacent to a loft welcome overnighters. Just for fun, an octagonal dining room was set on a corner, offering panoramic views for diners. From outside, the home traces the spaces they enclosed as they pleased, and the irregular outline serves to add architectural character and distinction.

A patio skirts the edge of the pond, where manmade waterfalls whisper, and a fire pit lies in wait for the perfect match.

Closer to home, a patio flanks the home, encompassing the radial bay dining room that adds architectural character from the outside, a panoramic view from within.

Light from within reveals the massive trusses that form the airy interior spaces. Picture windows filter views of the pond to the inhabitants, who more often than not find themselves relaxing by the water.

Upon approach, an architecturally unique home presents a façade of warm cedar shingles hand hewn log and stone. A slate colored roof is punctuated with cutout dormers and, foremost, a bump out angled to shelter an arched portico entry. Cedar logs also frame the three-bay garage, where custom doors replicate the swing-out entryways of historic carriage houses.

A tree trunk in the entry foyer blurs the line between indoors and out. The space is a beautiful introduction to the home, large enough to feature a display table where fresh flowers may sit one week, a bowl of pine cones the next.

Hand scribed enormous logs punctuate the great room, where a river stone wall marks the chimney and hearth, and the room is suffused with the honeyed glow of cedar wood. Red accents were added by the owners, sprinkled throughout the seating area, foyer, and kitchen beyond to tie the spaces together.

A light hand was used in selecting the window mullions, with only a sliver of crisscross, mission style, to frame the views.

A sweep of bar circles the kitchen, complete with swivel chairs and a foot rail for stay-all-evening comfort. The cook center is framed, fireplace style, with a wood surround complete with a mantel perfect for display, and on the other wall, glass-fronts continue the open feeling of the home.

His-and-hers baths in the master suite allowed for the expression of unique personalities. In hers, a soaking tub was snuggled as close to the outdoors as possible, right up to a picture window. A tree was even brought inside to help with the illusion.

A raised fireplace ensures that the flames can be enjoyed from under the covers, and creates a hearth wide enough to sit on. When the early birds come to get the worm, or the fish, or just a drink from the pond, the site is captured through glass sliders that keep the homeowners in constant touch with their lot's greatest amenity.

Invested in the Environment

So gently did the builders tread, that a small forest was preserved between front porch and garage, and trees were saved to within five feet of this new home. Not only do the trees owe the owners their lives, the owners are in debt for the shade, and the pleasing sense that their home has been decades in this space when in fact it was carefully crafted to fit their small family. Rising up from a small footprint, the rooms were carefully arranged to provide private spaces for two children on the first floor, a suite retreat for the parents on the second. At the back of the house, a great room juts out into the forest, with a cathedral ceiling and space for all to come together. Downstairs, a den provides a cozy family room, and a place where the children can escape when the adults are entertaining upstairs.

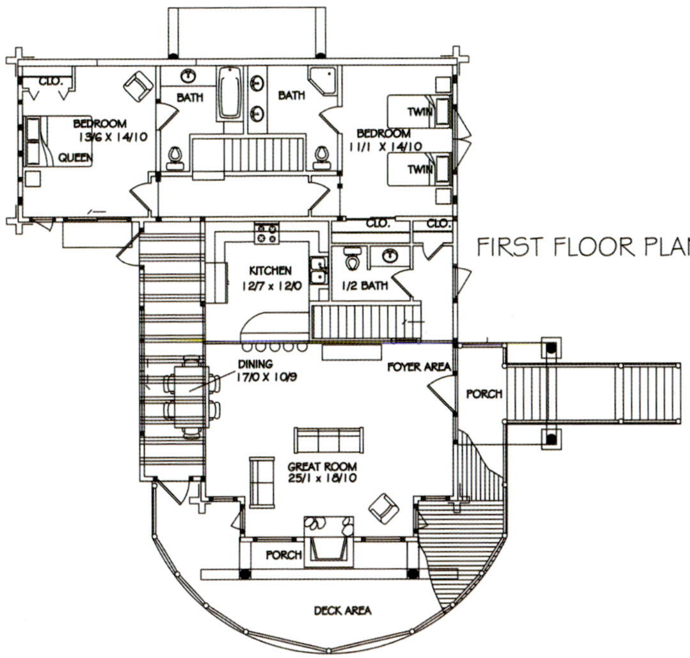

FIRST FLOOR PLAN

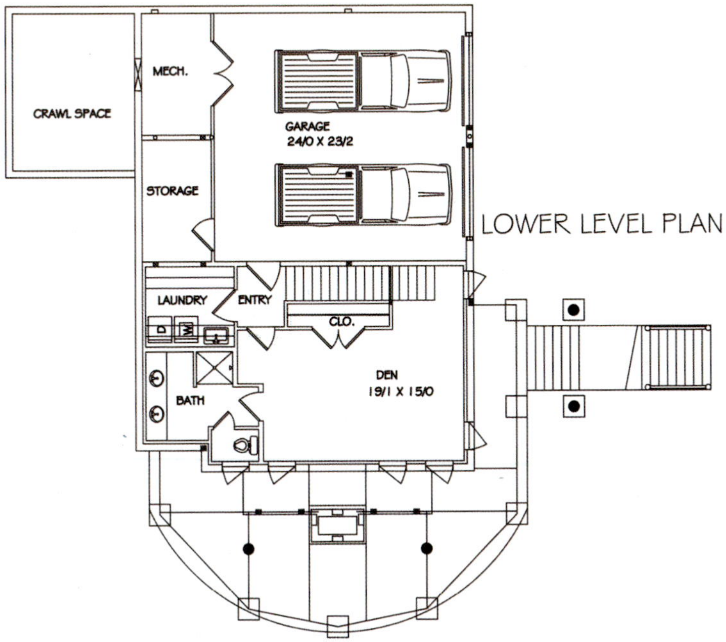

LOWER LEVEL PLAN

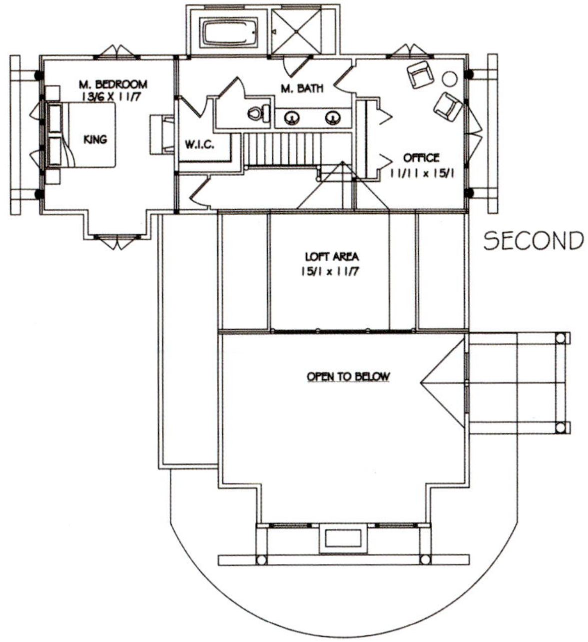

SECOND FLOOR PLAN

Stone, log, and weather-beaten boards were married for a magical home, a towering edifice that seems forever a part of its wooded place. A corrugated metal roof adds a final layer of texture to this fascinating structure.

(opposite)
An entry portico beckons from atop the home's stone base. By incorporating open-grate iron stairs, the owners saved themselves a lot of snow and leaf maintenance, and preserved the view of their impressive fieldstone foundation.

Fortress-like, the home rises from the forest and commands a view through the tree-tops. A deck extends prow-like into the woods, offering the owners a chance to relax and enjoy a bird's-eye view.

On an ell supporting the master bedroom, the reclaimed timber siding was repeated and completed with log framed square windows that add both light and privacy to the owner's lives.

The fieldstone was brought inside for a generous band of chimney extended up the great room wall. Wrought iron, too, was added to balcony and light fixtures, repeating the earthy elements used in the exterior décor. Comforting textiles and leathers introduce a human element to the mix, marrying the inhabitants with their wooded world.

Dark cherry and warm tile infuse the kitchen with color. The compact design minimizes the cook's need to travel between sink, cook unit, and fridge, and a counter provides the logical stopping point for casual meals.

Comfortable chairs and a bank of windows make the dining table a place to linger. Exposed log beams keep the inhabitants in touch with their support network. Just beyond, family photos personalize a hallway that connects the children's rooms.

Country charm suffuses a young woman's room, where French doors open to the rural world beyond.

A row of windows above the bed frames the art that these homeowner's invested in – their surroundings. Likewise, a window seat allows them to cuddle next to their chosen woodland world, and a picture window in the master bath allows bathers to soak it all in.

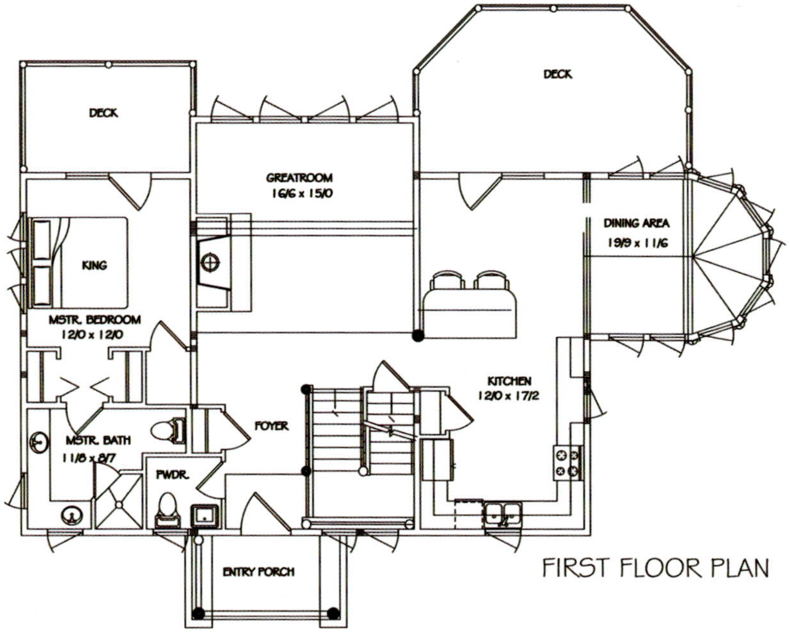

FIRST FLOOR PLAN

Plans Set in Motion

Their retirement dreams writ out in stone and wood, this handsome second home is a blueprint for the future set on the shores of a great lake. A ground level floor offers all the necessary amenities to the owners – kitchen and living areas, and expansive master suite, and decks that encompass the view they keep coming back for. Both upstairs and down, room has been set aside for friends and family to gather for vacations and holidays, where they can find their own privacy, and join their hosts in expansive central gathering areas. Lake breezes and the lap of watery waves promise pleasant days as summer rolls by, and come winter, ample storage space has been set aside so that the owners can stock up and simply ride out any inclement weather on the warm side of their picture windows. That's the plan, as they horde weekends toward retirement, the first major step already undertaken.

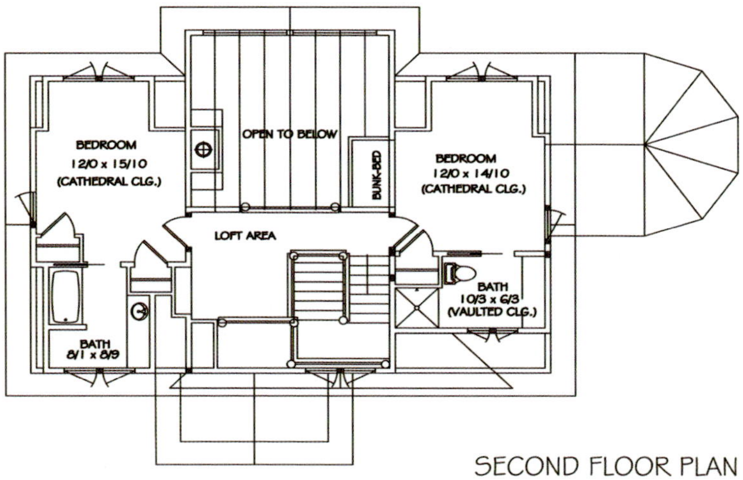

SECOND FLOOR PLAN

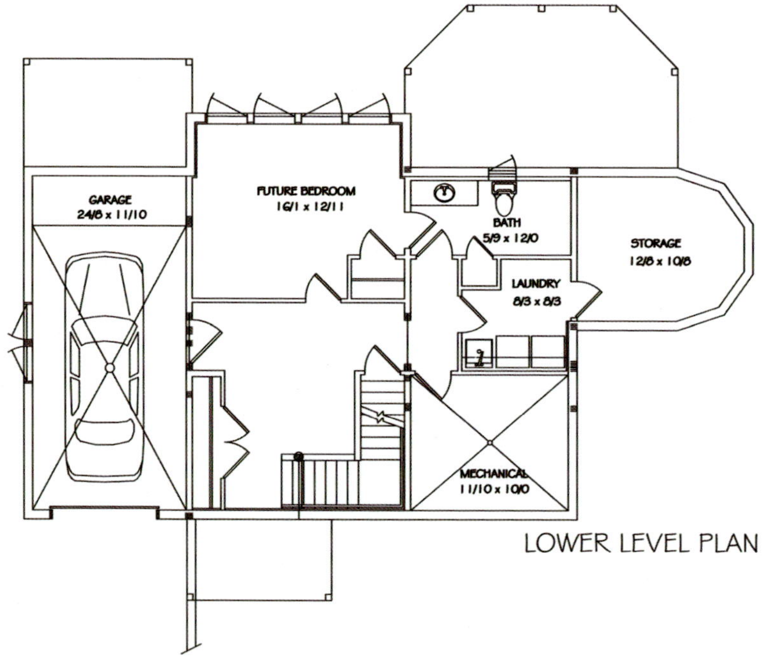

LOWER LEVEL PLAN

A barrel ceiling portico welcomes the owners home on Friday afternoons, and provides a place to linger as they tear themselves away come Sunday afternoon. The exterior combination of cedar log with cedar shake and stone accents makes a classically handsome statement.

Perched on the edge of a sandy descent to the beach, this destination home was designed to overlook the owner's sunset years. It is a welcoming retreat they enjoy in anticipation of these days.

A staircase scales the dunes, from deck to lakeshore. For those passing on the waters below, the log and shingle home appears a natural outgrowth in the forest.

A massive stone hearth plays second fiddle to the view by day, but can really light up the room at night. Above, cedar trusses bridge the great room, repeated in the window frame on the outside wall.

Two outside walls feed light to the kitchen, where black beadboard and granite counters provide punctuation within the airy space.

A unique, handcrafted baluster of stick - work frames the balcony overlooking the great room. This lofty reading nook is a perfect roost for observing the hand scribed log framework of the structure, as well as the two-story view beyond.

Thrust out from the structure, a radial bay dining room affords a panoramic view.

Once again, black has been used to add accent to the master suite, where a unique stick canopy frames the bed, and granite tops his-and-her sinks in the lavatory.

Guest rooms were comfortably furnished within the varied architecture of the eaves, and windows offered to open the rooms to the million-dollar view.

Rocky Mountain Retreat

Front to back, this is an extraordinary home. Lovers of timber frame, the homeowners released their wildest fantasies in commissioning a home supported by enormous arched collar braces pierced by king posts of equal immensity and stature. The arched theme carries through from front to back as the timbers trace the outline of the home's cathedral-like central great room area. Beautifully chinked log bump-outs flank this open space on both sides, providing a private master suite in one wing, a garage and mudroom in the other. Downstairs, the winged shape allows for two gathering rooms and three bedrooms, each with private baths.

An entry spills into a sheltered foyer, extended in cozy greeting beyond the massive central room within.

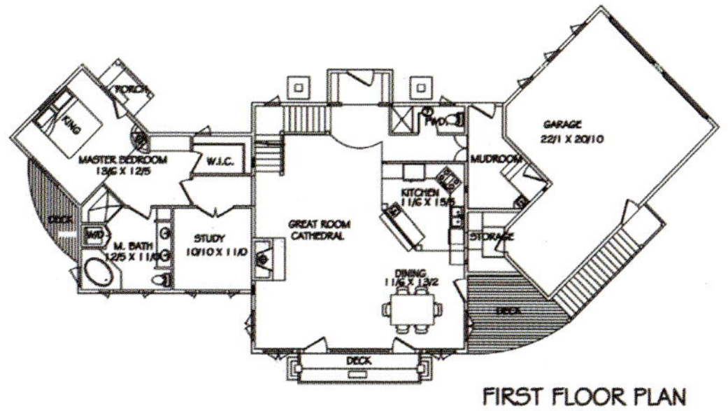

FIRST FLOOR PLAN

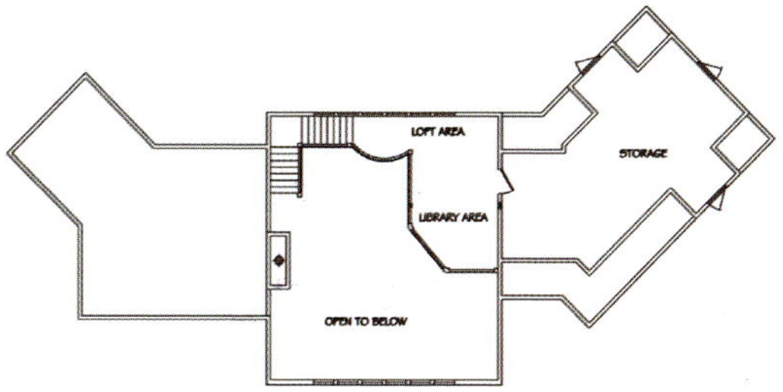

SECOND FLOOR PLAN

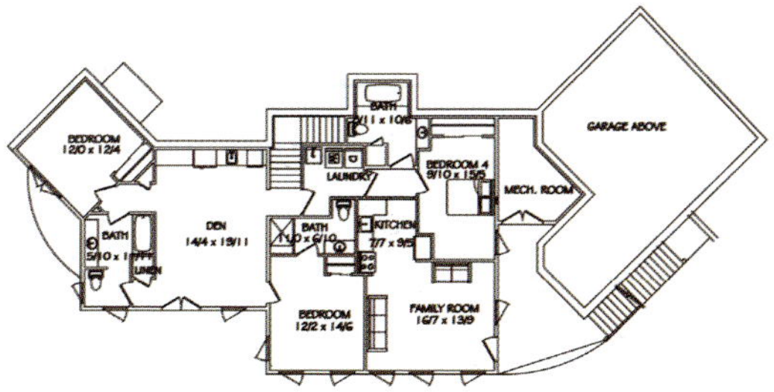

LOWER LEVEL PLAN

A benefit to its Rocky Mountain nest, this log-winged wonder is a jewel on the landscape.

A small loft was created over the entryway to allow the owners and visiting admirers a chance to get close to the amazing woodwork that supports this structure.

Various angles help to illustrate the wonder of the great room space, inspiring in its height and construction, uplifting in the amount of light that floods the interior. Doors and windows form a thin line between inside and out, allowing the occupants a sense of connectedness, albeit sheltered from sub-zero temperatures.

The kitchen space is defined by the overhang of a loft space, and the decorative curve of a bar counter and stools.

The master suite enjoys a private wing of the home, and the same quality of lofty timber-framed spaces and light as the central great room.

A rug and the ever-present views establish a dining area, where ten can pull up chairs to an enormous table.

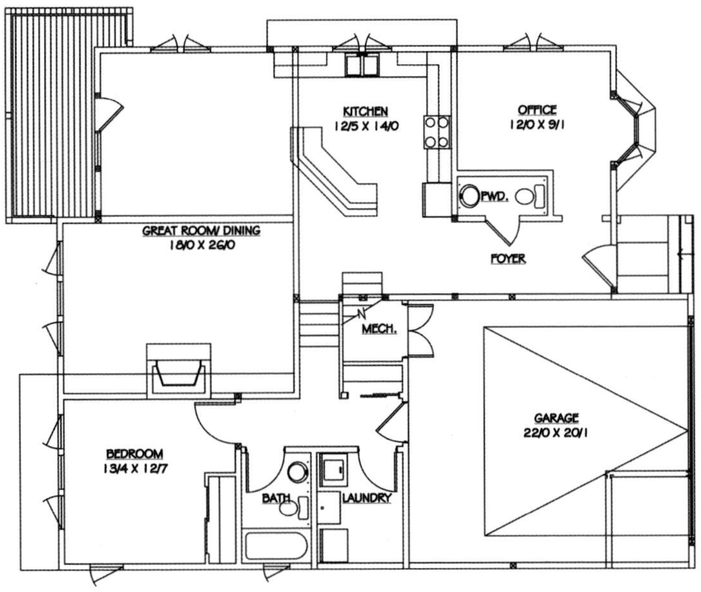

FIRST FLOOR PLAN

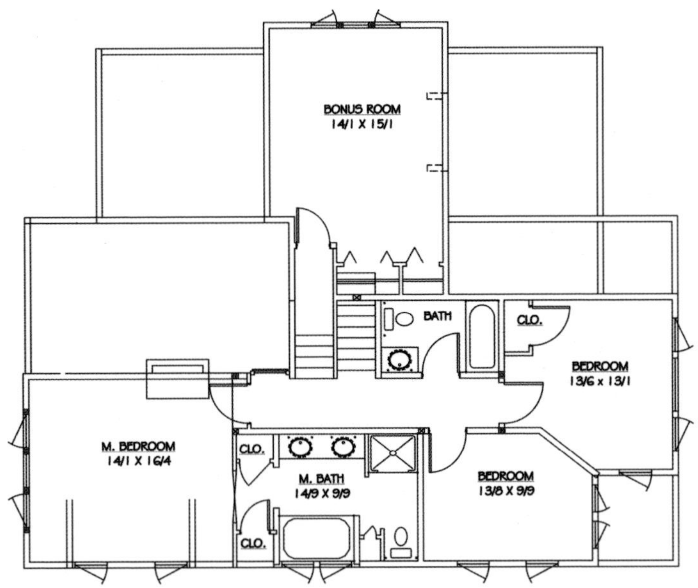

LOWER LEVEL PLAN

Provisioned in Style

Days might go by when this family doesn't leave the driveway. The driveway is long, town is far, and the snow gets deep. That's why this home design started with a home office, so work can get done no matter the weather. Moreover, when the roads are clear, work can come home in the form of visiting clients and co-workers. A front foyer can funnel people into either the office or the more intimate family areas. There' is a guest room on the lower entry level, and the family's private bedrooms are all located on a "first-floor" balcony. That extra bedroom comes in handy in the event of an exceptionally big blanket of snow – an extra space where family members can seclude themselves. Of course, snow doesn't stop this outdoorsy clan from venturing outside. Sledding and snowmobiling starts at their doorstep, and wildlife and scenic wonders beckon through every expansive picture window.

An eave extension shelters the front entry, holding drifts at bay during the heaviest of winter's snow falls.

Set amidst a backdrop of snow-capped mountains, this custom timber frame and log home is its own scenic wonder. Rugged timbers, stone, and cedar shake shingles befit the context, and frame up a handsome home worthy of its setting.

A great sledding hill lies just beyond the back door, overlooked by the expansive window and artful angles of the home.

A split stacked stone fireplace warms a seating area within the great room. Again, triangle windows are repeated on the back of the house for design consistency, and overall "wow" effect.

An entry foyer directs visitors to either a home office or the family spaces beyond. Designed for privacy, it is artfully lit by two triangular panes in keeping with the overall design of the home.

A bar counter creates an inviting barrier between kitchen and great room areas, and the dining area is likewise connected. Family members and guests feel free to find their comfort spots within the space, without separating from the group.

These windows are seductive, inviting an easy slip into a daydream for those enchanted by the view.

Earthy tones soften the bedrooms and baths, creating comfort zones replete with color, texture, and western wilderness themes that envelope the family.

All Downhill

This little four-bedroom, five-bath log "cabin" in the Rockies is the launching pad for ski parties hosted seven months a year by a family of enthusiasts. They packed their private lodge with plenty of space to display their loved things, a grand gathering area, a sequestered recreation room, and lots and lots of view. There's plenty of space for friends to feel comfortable, complete with a private room and bath. As a warm up before heading to the resorts, there's even skiing right out the back door, for those willing to hike back up the mountainside. The worst part is finding enough time to be here!

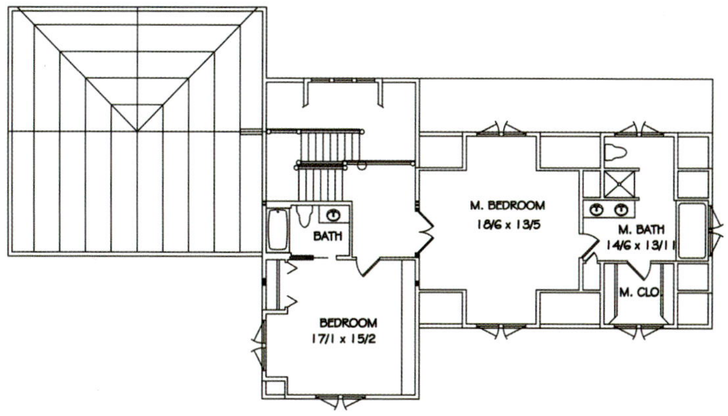

SECOND FLOOR PLAN

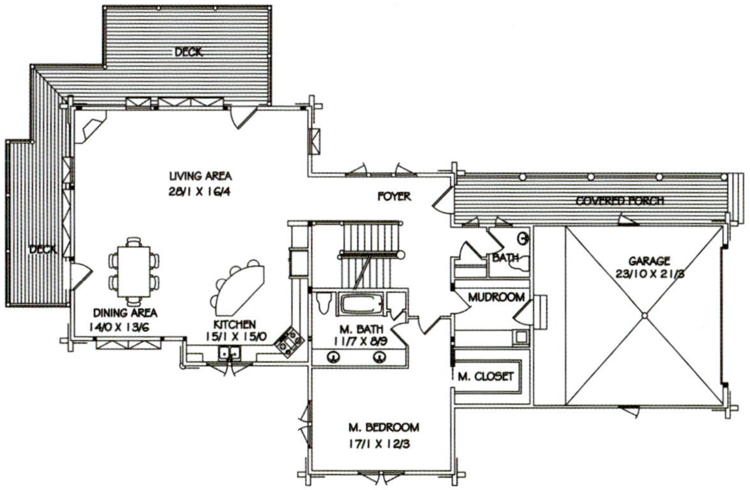

FIRST FLOOR PLAN

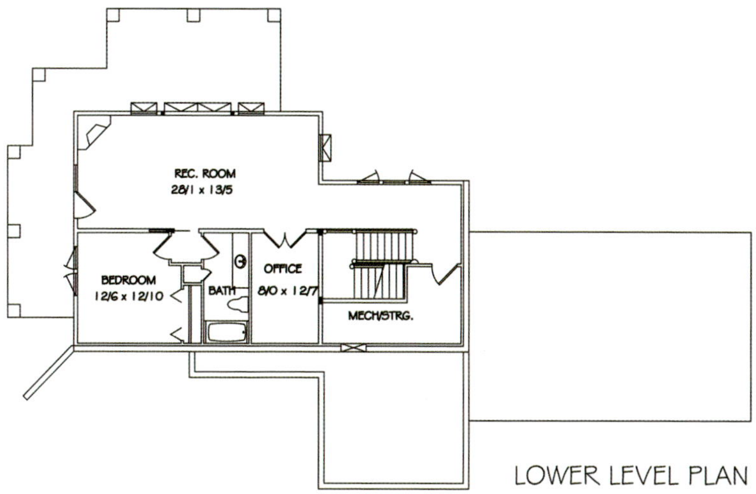

LOWER LEVEL PLAN

Log home construction was the obvious choice for this skiing lodge in the mountains. Cedar timbers will assure that, like the more simple cabins built hundreds of years ago by mountain pioneers, this structure will stand up to whatever nature might throw its way.

Three black diamonds on a sign indicate the steep slope over which the home looks. These are folks anxious to experience each fresh powder, and their home is the perfect launching point for the resorts nearby. Those willing to hike back up can, indeed, venture out the back door! A fireplace awaits their return, ready to warm them while they relate their adventures.

An entry foyer creates a warm winter welcome, where youthful enthusiasm spills over into antique appointments.

Comfy stools, warm food, and tales of the outdoors fill this kitchen corner after sunset.

A huge plate glass picture window backs the dining table, creating an outdoor environment inside on days when the party can't move to the deck.

A small breakfast nook on the other side of the great room is a favorite card table after hours.

A master bath suite is packed with country charm, the shower stall inconspicuous behind a frosty wall of glass block.

Fishing memorabilia adorns this bedroom, a virtual museum in addition to a restful place among the eaves.

The outdoors comes in again for this guest room, where antiques and country accents imbue a room of hand hewn logs with color and charm.

Western Apparel

A rugged log home was outfitted for contemporary life, using today's standards for scale and comfort while echoing the aesthetics of an earlier time. ranch gear, rich leather, and Native American motifs were salted throughout the home, where exposed logs and hand-crafted details attest to the preservation of traditions. Three compact stories keep this home energy efficient, while providing a central well, where light is filtered into the house and all its radial rooms. A walk-out basement gets its share of the light with a large family room area flanked by his and hers art and shop rooms. Above, a great room commands the first floor, its height extending to the peaked cathedral ceiling. Flanking it on one side are the kitchen and dining room, on the other, the master bedroom and bath. A generous entry provides a grand first impression to the massive central space. Overlooking all is a loft and office area, with a large library to store the collection of two book lovers.

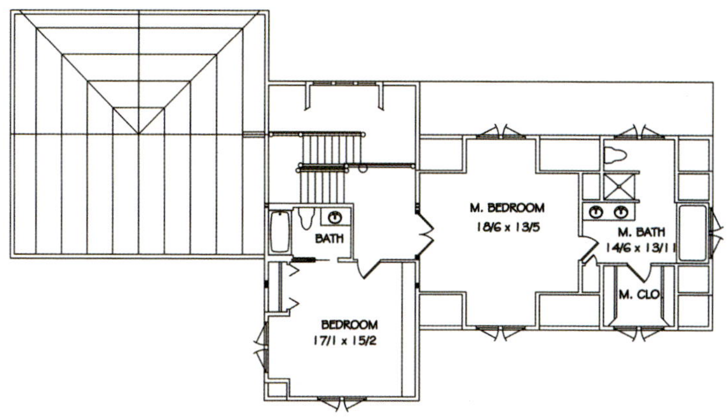

SECOND FLOOR PLAN

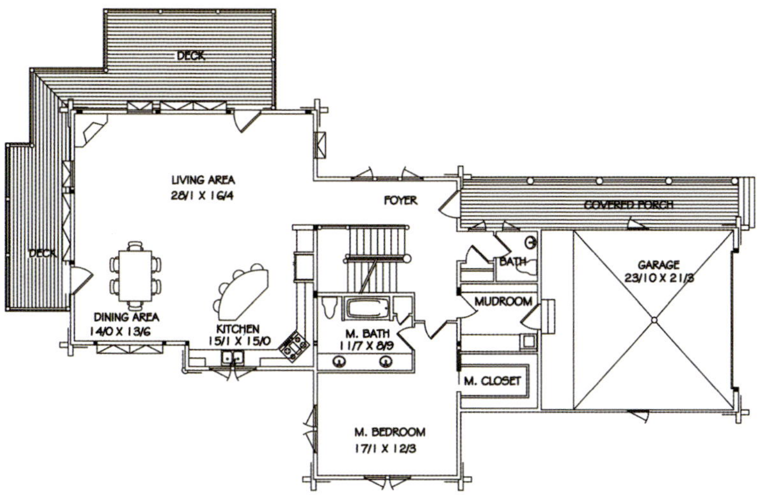

FIRST FLOOR PLAN

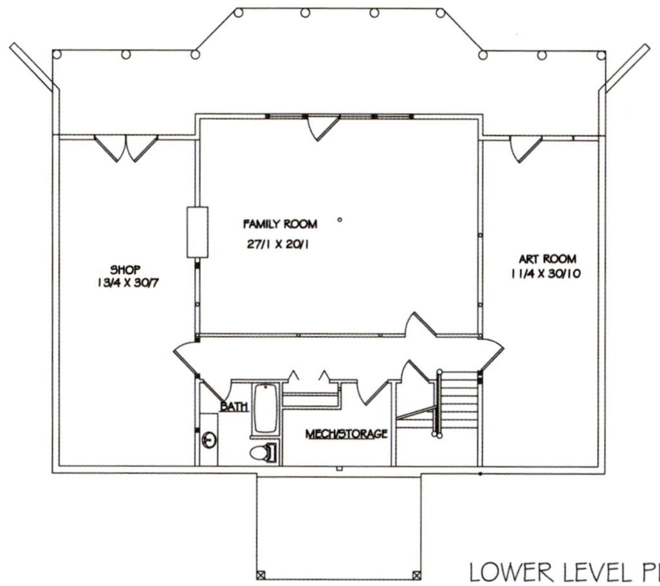

LOWER LEVEL PLAN

Logs and light make up the profile of this handsome home, commanding a hilltop view and standing as a fortress to the sometimes harsh elements of the West. Dormer windows feed light to office and library alcoves in the loft, while the central peak floods light into the great room on the first floor.

An impressive entryway provides visual and foot access to the great room beyond. Beside it, a U-shaped staircase with open steps leads to a commanding loft office, trimmed with a twig rail system.

Western and equestrian motifs adorn the great room, illuminated by two stories of picture window. Great blocks of stone underlined by ashlar form a focal point around the hearth.

Light cabinetry and countertop form a smooth counterpoint to the exposed log walls surrounding it in the dining area and great room. Antique wood doors open to the dining room beyond.

The western motif predominates in the dining room, where a yoke and lariat adorn the log wall, along with framed artwork.

A rugged bedstead reflects the Spanish influence upon western design, and seems most fitting in a room hewn from rugged timbers.

A generous allowance of sunlight was apportioned for those who want to linger in a broad soaking tub.

A Water Park

Blessed with a beautiful lake view, and surrounded by running water, this rural gem offers its owners a daily dose of beauty and serenity at every turn. A dream home from front door to back, their custom log home is a spacious and expansive family space, where they frequently entertain friends and family. A bridge welcomes those guests to a covered portico and impressive foyer, beyond which await a great room and sunlit dining room designed to host large parties. When the crowd overflows, there's an expansive deck just beyond, that puts guests in touch with a beautiful lake view at the foot of the landscaped lawn.

A welcoming approach crosses water and stone enroute to two other inviting elements – wood and light.

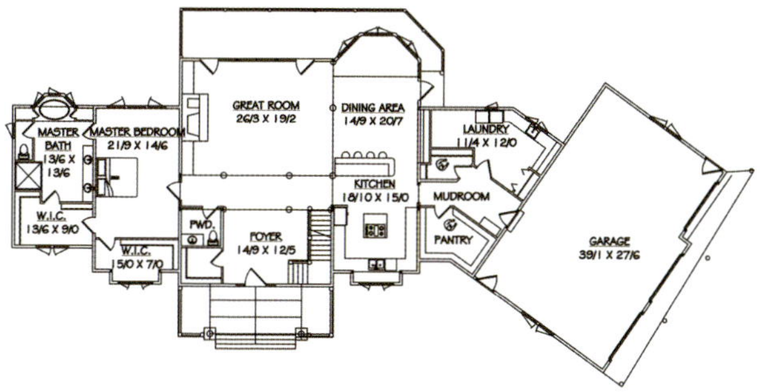

FIRST FLOOR PLAN

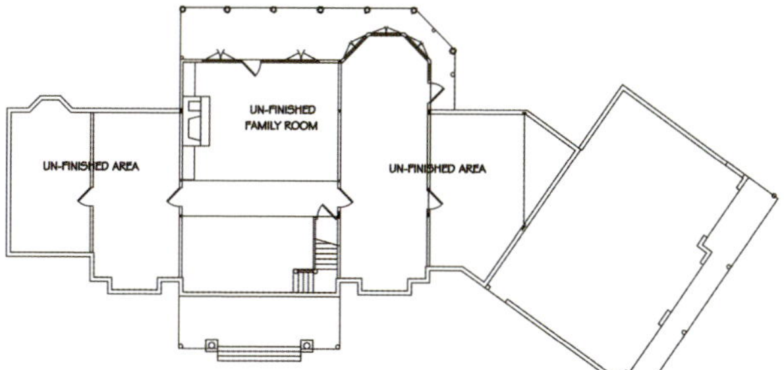

LOWER LEVEL PLAN

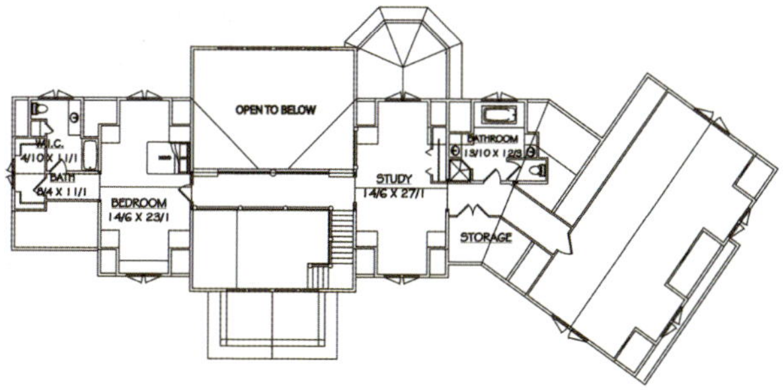

SECOND FLOOR PLAN

A lakeside property demands a home appropriate to its beauty. This custom log home fills the bill.

Stonework forms the footers for the elevated deck, and matching rock forms retaining walls that establish inviting overlooks for the lake views.

Just beyond the deck footers, a private spa simmers, seemingly sprung from the earth itself. For close friends and family a dip in this heated pool provides the perfect ending to a perfect evening.

An octagonal gazebo with a stone base, cedar pillars, and cozy fireplace creates an outdoor room at the periphery of the patio.

An A-frame entry luminates a foyer designed to impress first time arrivals, and inspire daily awe in the owners. Huge king log trusses support the interior great room, and an open stairwell gives glimpses both up and down to the spaces beyond.

Leather, stained glass, stone, and northern white cedar bespeak distinction in a great room that is both comforting in its appointments and awe inspiring in its upper stretches.

An extended counter forms a bar with stools along the periphery of the generous kitchen, easily converted into a buffet counter. Within, a large inner island creates a great workstation.

A half radial bay cedar extension carries the dining room into the backyard, creating a lengthy space to seat guests, and a semi-circle of windows to help digest the view.

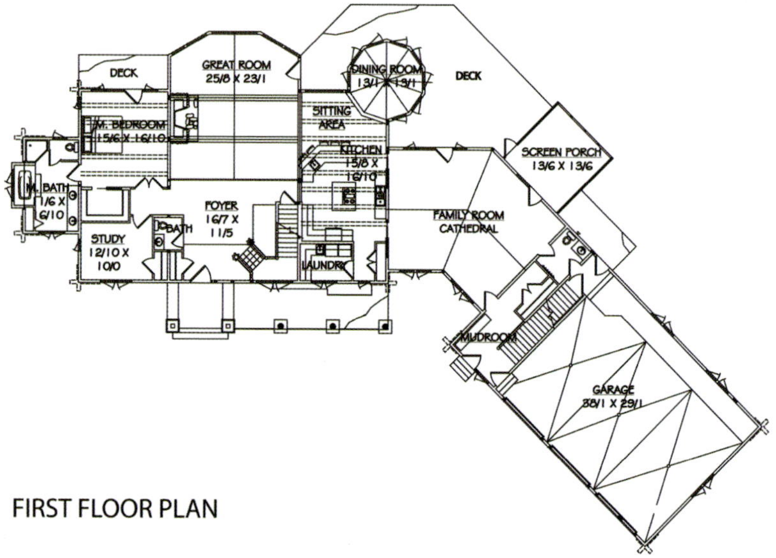

FIRST FLOOR PLAN

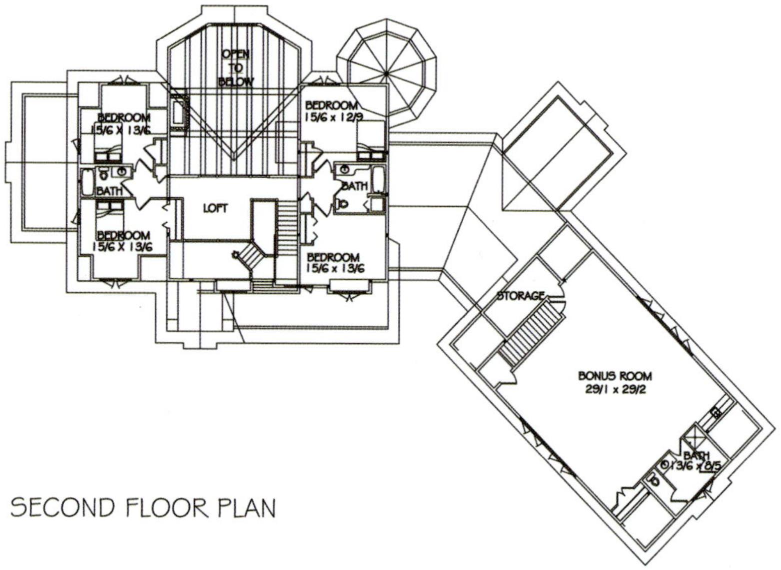

SECOND FLOOR PLAN

Wooded Wonderland

A lakefront, a lot of trees, and a burbling brook were what mattered most when this family started drawing up plans to live on this pastoral prize. To fit within this context, they chose a home that outwardly reflected its landscaping, clad in cedar shingles, and overhung by eaves painted as green as the fir boughs that towered over them. Within, a central log truss system allowed them to create the great open spaces necessitated by four growing children and their friends – a family room and a living room both in place for the sometimes divided interests along generation and gender lines. Wings constructed of traditional notched logs were set up for more intimate spaces within the rambling structure. A large lower level was also created but left unfinished so that as the future needs and budget grew, more space would be available for use. A bonus room over the garage was also plumbed for a bath, making it a great guest suite.

A flagstone walkway winds its way through a beautiful landscape of rhododendrons and hosta to a welcoming portico.

A stone bridge traverses a winding stream on the approach to this handsome property. Besides forming the charming bridge from roadside parking to front door for guests, it is also the owner's favorite preamble to a stroll along the quiet neighboring roads.

Crisscrossing the landscaping, meandering streams and stone bridges form a park-like setting surrounding this cedar home. Many trees were carefully preserved to shield the home from harsh summer sun, and to maintain the fairyland atmosphere.

Patio encompasses two levels of backyard, allowing family members to immerse themselves into the wooded environment, where a constant background of waterfall music provides entertainment.

A great room serves as the central gathering place for the family, next to food, dining, the decks, and an overlook of the wonderful, wooded backyard and lake beyond. King trusses bear a cathedral ceiling and support a wall of windows, allowing those inside to experience a closeness to the towering trees that frame the sky just beyond these walls.

Innovative use of space is found in the angled wing between kitchen and garage, forming recreational, dining and gathering spaces for the family. Cedar purlins and end match paneling grace the ceiling of this fortressed family room.

A screened porch off the family room forms a transition between this common gathering spot and the patio beyond.

Mom can serve dinner to her entire brood along this great stretch of kitchen counter. Her kitchen is kept open and uncluttered thanks to a spacious pantry closet in the rear.

Eight angles of a circular dining room extend beyond the exterior walls for a panoramic view. The sunlit radial bay cedar dining room is a magnet for visitors, offering a 270 - degree overlook.

A master suite on the first floor is finished with cedar floor and ceiling, with white walls for variation. A pedestal tub in the bathroom suite sets the stage for a leisurely respite, removed from the main living areas of the home.

Different Strokes

No luxuries were spared in this lakeshore property for two. Soaring ceilings of exposed beams tower overhead, while at eye level, enormous windows let in light, breeze, and views of a private lake. As if one body of water wasn't enough, the couple planned an indoor exercise pool and massaging whirlpool, all part-and-parcel of their expansive floorplan.

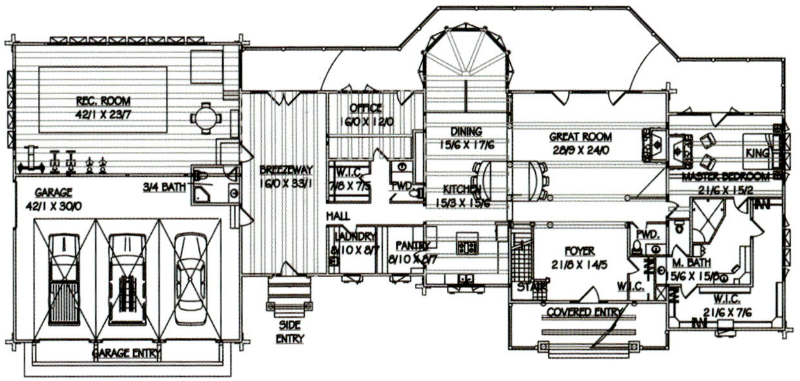

FIRST FLOOR PLAN

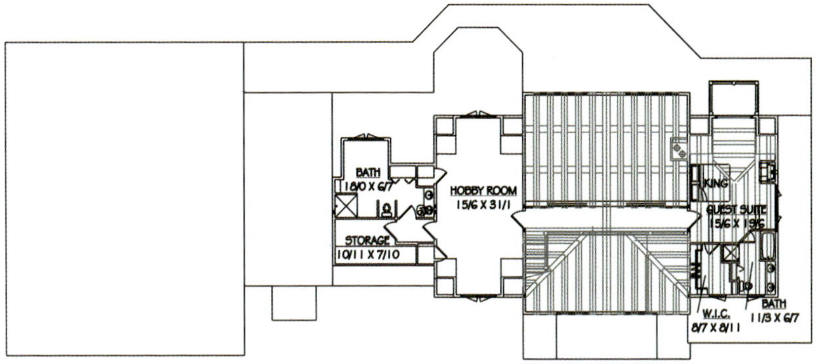

SECOND FLOOR PLAN

Hand-hewn logs give a new twist on an old favorite in this home's porch railing. The façade is composed of half-round logs; overhead, a large cedar king truss supports the entryway.

From across the lake, the home is sizable and inviting, like a gated community's lodge, and with its green roof and low profile, the home nestles unobtrusively into the field and trees surrounding it.

The back of the home features hand hewn log walls and more custom log railings around the porch's perimeter, as well as an array of dynamic rooflines that break up the dominating horizontal planes.

A sunroom outcropping emerges onto the extra-wide deck. Green trim around windows and the sliding doors help unite the roof with the mainframe of the home. In the distance, the large, stone gazebo draws guests out onto the patio.

A chef's paradise can be found within the gazebo, where an outdoor kitchen and grill are built-in beside a fieldstone fireplace and intimate dining area. A roof broad enough to capture grill and hearth heat makes this a great outdoor dining space in warm or cool weather. Two chairs are perfectly positioned on the earthy concrete patio for sunbathing and taking in views of the private lake.

Inside, the great room is overseen by enormous exposed structural logs, arranged in wagon-wheel designs that span the full width of the room. Between, an antler chandelier sets the "cabin" mood. The logs are echoed in a natural log mantle on a massive fieldstone chimney. Pillows in a myriad of stripes, spots, and fringes pepper the sofa and armchairs, and an oriental rug defines the space.

French doors open the great room out onto the deck, while a hunting rifle acts as a slim decoration perfect for embellishing the window's narrow panes.

A western motif dominates the bar area, where bronco silhouettes set the scene on the chair backs, a rifle hangs over a flat-panel television, and off to the side a western saddle becomes a piece of art.

A sitting area with flagstone floor features half-log walls and high ceilings, furnished by a rich leather sofa and chair and a gaming table with an ideal view. In good lakefront tradition, a fisherman finds his home on the end table and fish create matching art for the wall. French doors lead to the deck and gazebo.

Raised panel cabinet doors nearly cover the walls in this ultra-functional kitchen of pale greens, browns, and subtle pinks. Sidle up to a pale green island with marbled, bar-height counter on one of the tall leather stools; enjoy the soft greens and interesting textures of a custom brick backsplash, and find ample preparation and serving surfaces on a perimeter of deep gray marble countertops.

Beneath a peaked ceiling spanned by large log crossbeams, a long dining table sits atop a space-defining oriental rug. At each juncture of log and windowpane, heavy, textured drapery is gathered to let in the sunlight and the great views.

Upstairs, the catwalk is railed by a twig banister, offering a delicate web design inspired by nature. Beneath the angular ceiling peaks, nooks and crannies offer hiding places where a comfy reading chair and cabin-style lamp offer a quick getaway.

In the master bathroom, strategically placed raised-panel cabinets in a clean white shade create handy storage places beside each of the sinks. Sunk into angled granite countertops, these twin bowls allow two to primp at once. Behind, a glass-block wall keeps the shower bright while maintaining privacy.

A custom sink and vanity is finished with an antique gold faucet and a beveled-edge oval mirror.

The master bedroom features another stunning fieldstone fireplace, which faces two leather armchairs angled inward. Tongue-and-groove cedar ceiling panels reflect light into the room, and half-round logs create an elegant wallpaper. A set of French doors leads out onto a private deck.

For the active homeowners, an in-ground lap pool and corner whirlpool are positioned beneath an impressive timber-frame window, warming the water year round with passive solar heat.

Beneath a peaked ceiling and walls of horizontal cedar paneling that keep sunlight moving throughout the room, a cabin-style log and iron bed waits to welcome guests in this second bedroom.

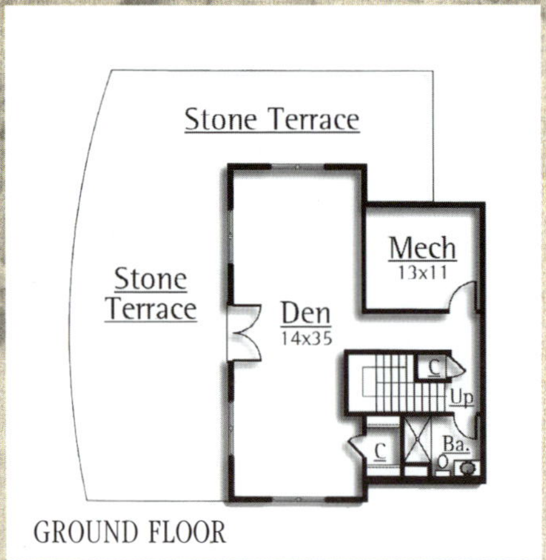

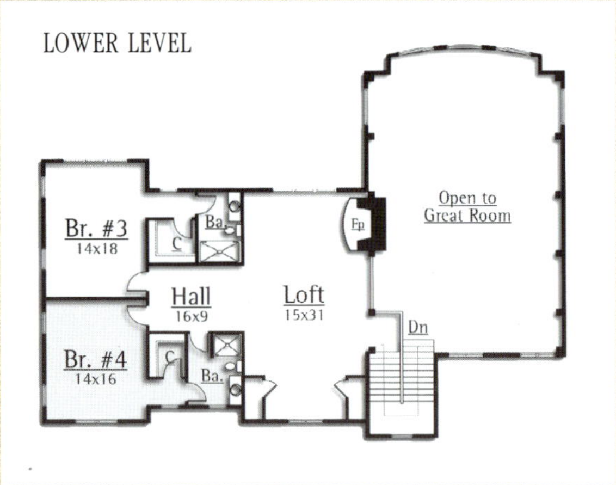

Blue Ridge Lodge

Courtesy of MossCreek Designs

Seven gables are easily apparent from below, as this elegant cedar home perches on a forested eastern hillside. This two-story mansion crowns an inviting wooded slope, with welcoming open windows and a sheltered entryway. Closer examination reveals the warmth of glowing fireplaces, sunny porches, intimate gathering areas, and reading corners that welcome guests of all ages with open arms.

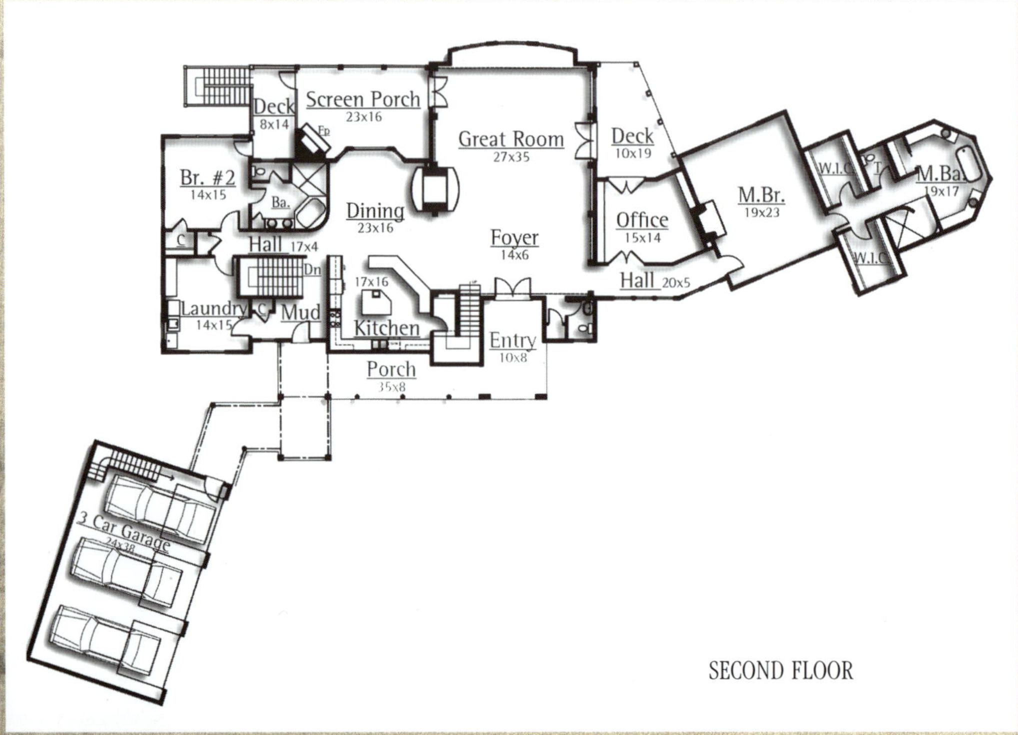

The front facade demonstrates unparalleled attention to detail, each peaked roof punctuated by a bow of timber and a wagon-wheel motif, and each jutting, unexpected dormer covered with a choice of stone, shingle, tongue-and-groove paneling or half-round log. Beneath a deep covered porch, a custom glass door previews the continuation of custom details within.

The reclaimed timber entry and twig railing trim are accents to the cedar shake and board & baton finishes on this aerie mountain home. Custom timber eaves at the peak of each gable draw the eye to this distinctive architecture.

Rear porches featuring natural stick railing and plenty of wicker seating beneath a tall stone hearth speak of the inhabitant's passion for outdoor spaces, and their love of the incredible view from their Adirondack retreat, resplendant with all the colors of nature.

Signature soaring peaks and dramatic windows cover the back of the home, framing the mountaintop interior view.

The far wall of windows is positioned for a perfect view of eye-level mountains behind this hilltop home. Above the sitting area, wagon-wheel beam designs made of thick exposed wood span the room.

In the great room, a magnificent two-way fireplace sits in a centerpiece. Ornate details in the hand-carved, wrap-around wooden mantle, the complex oriental rug, and hand-forged wrought iron balusters offer the eye a few intricate focal points in a room of extraordinary size and grandeur.

A gourmet kitchen features beautiful raised-panel cabinetry around almost the entire perimeter and a granite counter capping the cabinets that build a curved fourth wall. A lovely olive and ochre window valance coordinates with the kitchen's crown molding, reminding us that bravery and risk-taking when choosing color can be very rewarding.

The hand-carved mantle featured in the great room wraps around the two-way hearth, leading to a small sitting area and informal dining space that are warmed by the shared fire.

The formal dining room boasts some of the best views in the home. A glass pedestal holds a bronze bald eagle that nicely finishes the mountain majesty behind it.

A magnet for the young set, an upstairs balcony holds a pool table, ready for a spirited round, and a neighboring home theater and game table ensures fun for all.

A free-standing tub is set in an angular outcropping for a private spa experience at home. The eye follows tall windows behind it upwards to a luxurious valance, then to a graduated recessed ceiling with wood trim, and rests upon a lotus chandelier of delicate pink petals and ambient light.

Next door, the master bedroom suite finds a fireplace taking center stage, with a unique combination of a rustic stone hearth and elegant wood mantle painted a clean, country white.

In a second bedroom, tall windows break up deep green walls, creating wide swaths of light and allowing a nearly seamless mountain view. A wrought iron and wood bed is blanketed with floral clusters that incorporate the walls' hunter green shade.

High on a Mountain

A property blessed with an enviable perch challenged its owners to create a home equal in stature. Their choice of timber frame construction reflected the desire for a home with interior spaces as inspiring as those surrounding it. To achieve cathedral ceilings, lofty spaces, and an open floor plan, massive cedar timbers were put to work to frame the new creation. The art of this timeless construction style is reflected upon arrival, with a curved collar brace supporting the entry portico. Inside, the same semi-circular woodwork is echoed across the expanse of a great room, and ripples are carried through in other round-top windows on flanking dormers.

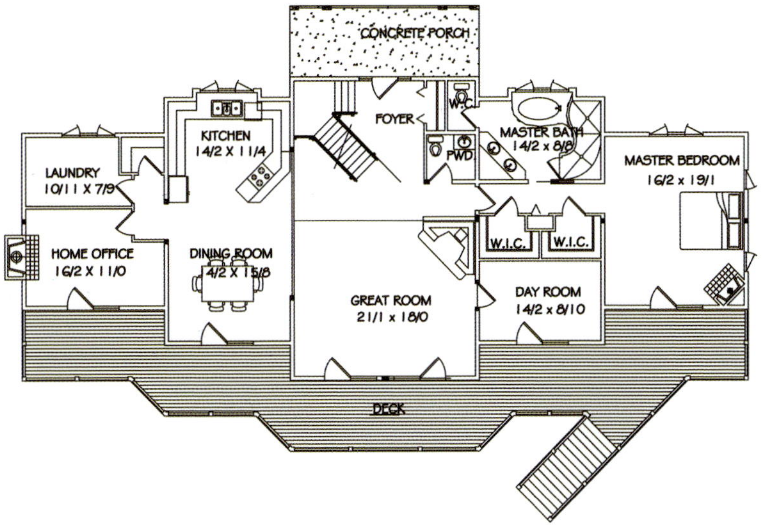

FIRST FLOOR PLAN

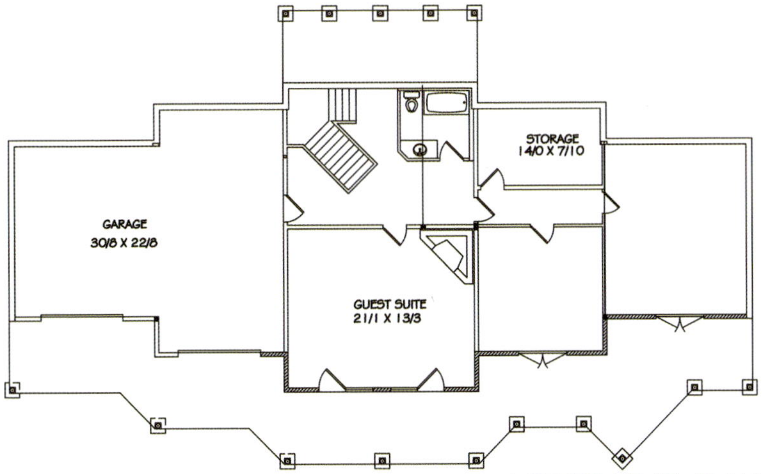

LOWER LEVEL PLAN

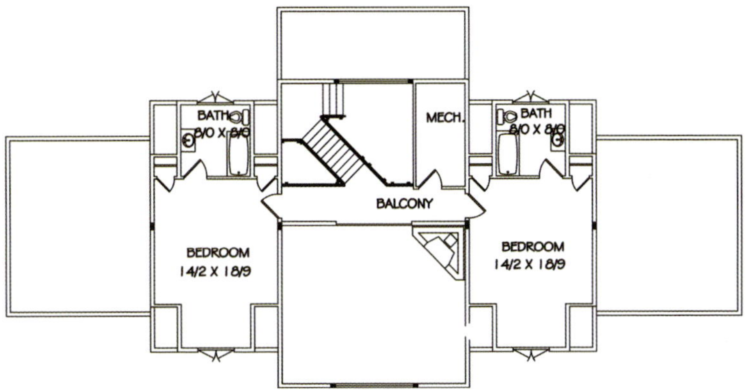

SECOND FLOOR PLAN

(opposite)
Gingerly setting footings in the forest, this home was situated to both command a mountaintop view, and preserve many of the towering pines that predate this remote Arizona mountain settlement.

Decks run the length of the home in back, where every first floor room offers an exit toward the view, and even the lower level has full slider doors that open toward the wilderness.

A light-filled entry foyer immerses new arrivals into the expansive open spaces of this timber-frame structure. Free of walls, the living spaces in the central portion of the home allowed the homeowners freedom to arrange their gathering places to suit their lifestyles. An open staircase acts as a natural divider, along with a catwalk between the entry and the great room beyond.

The semi-circle of a collar beam commands the cathedral space of the great room, illuminated by a reflected shape in the gable window beyond. Neutral tones in the décor, and tabletop lighting add a natural feel for the cozy living space established next to the massive stone hearth.

Ready to entertain, the social homeowners made sure they had wine ready to serve, and a kitchen big enough to accommodate the inevitable crush of friends and family gathering around a central, granite-topped island. Tucked under the open staircase right next door, bar stools flank an elevated beverage table for those who want to be near the action. This nook has become the owner's favorite spot to read the morning paper and sip a cup of coffee or tea.

A dining room table is easily expanded to accommodate guests. However, weather permitting, the food and friends tend to slip through the sliding glass doors to the deck beyond.

Separate from the living areas, a home office commands a private wing of the home.

The master suite opens to the deck, and a sunrise overlook on the mountain. A gas fireplace in one corner, an easy chair in the other, the owners enjoy their light and airy room long after the sun rises.

A handsome guest suite on the lower level offers both privacy and a dose of sunshine and view, with doors to a patio.

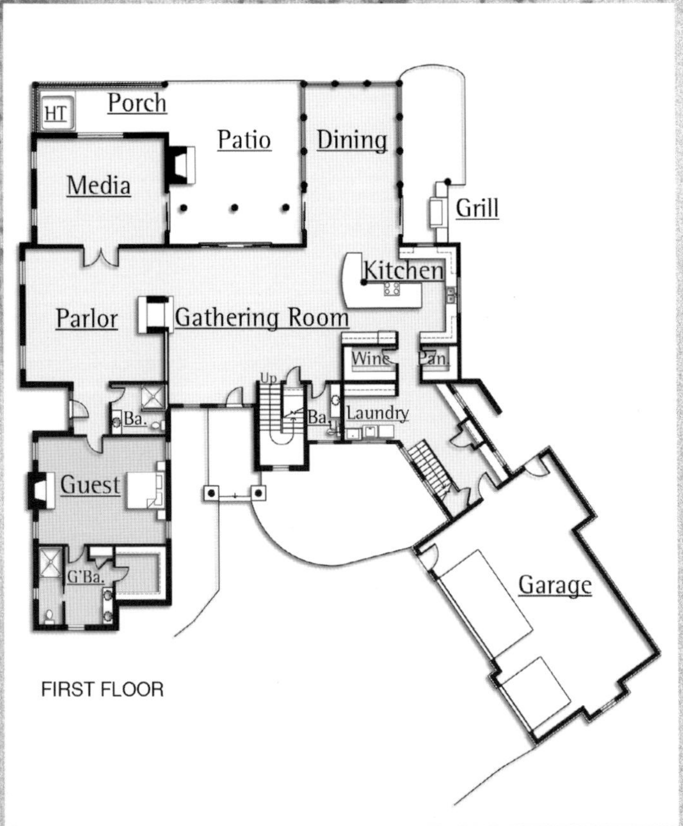

Romantic Rendezvous

Courtesy of MossCreek Designs

When their children grew up, moved away, and began to have children of their own, this couple knew it was time to construct their dream home: a couple's cabin that spared no luxury for the principle inhabitants, but still made room to entertain returning sons and daughters and their children. The plans include an extraordinary master suite with dream bathroom, private study, and other rooms intended just for them, but integrated a media room, guest room with exceptional bathroom and closet, and a separate, pajama-party-ready bunk room that sleeps at least four in a separate wing of the house – perfect for the giggling group of grandchildren who come to stay the weekend. When construction finished and the couple entered their new home, it was as if the honeymoon had begun all over again.

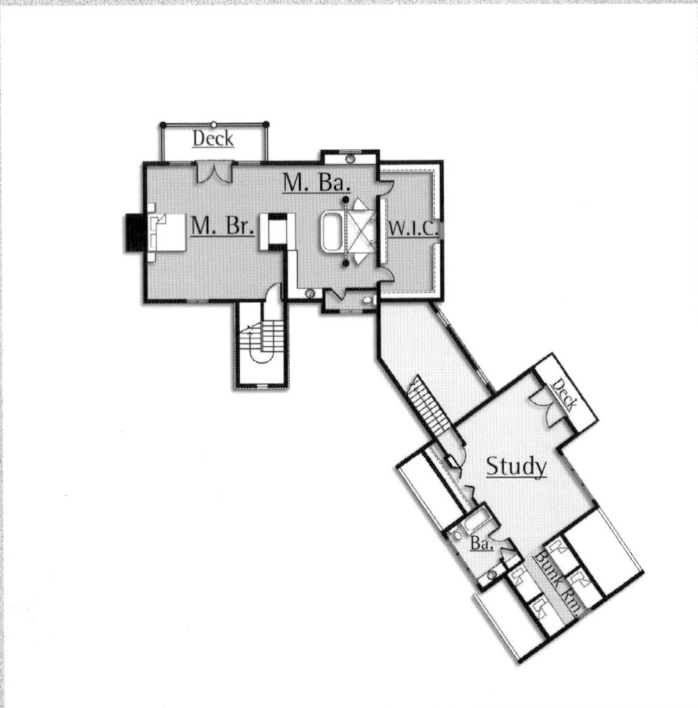

A set of solid double doors sits beneath a deep overhang of extra-large natural cedar logs. From under the eaves of roofs, the log trim is repeated all over the façade. Board and baton finish the second level, providing textural relief against the majestic stonework and windows of this fortress-like personal retreat.

An expansive backyard performs double duty with plenty of sunny garden solitude for a couple to cultivate herbs and flowers, and a shady open lawn beyond for picnicking and backyard games with visiting family. A custom cedar log rail system delights the eye with pattern and texture.

The main living room is furnished with leather chairs, bronze sculptures, and oversized flower arrangements in unique vases. A rustic flagstone floor unites the grays and red-browns of the room's furnishings. On the far wall, a hearth serves many purposes, with a peek-through fireplace cut into the lower right corner and shelving and cabinets built into the top and left. Stained thick cedar log emerges cut-side-out as a unique textured mantle. Expansive French doors and floor-to-ceiling windows fill this room with light. Cedar purlins and trim abound, retaining the architectural integrity of the home.

Through the arched doorway, a parlor with mini-bar waits, ready to entertain, with a flat-panel television above the mantle. Next door, a second media room offers simultaneous options when family is visiting. Adults are connected to the goings on among the children, with large double doors between the two television rooms to allow close monitoring by the parents, or a sound barrier for those who want to converse in the next room.

A breakfast bar is lit by stylish café lighting at the edge of this gourmet kitchen filled with stone and deep wood accents. A unique mid-room vent over an island range keeps the chef from being confined to a wall-facing stove.

What sophisticated couple's cabin would be complete without a winecellar? Behind a wooden door with a cutout of intricate wrought iron details, custom shelving and cabinetry create spaces for a discerning palette's fine collection.

The dining area stands ready for dinner party after dinner party. A peaked ceiling is spanned by oversized exposed logs, and around the perimeter, a wall of windows speaks of al fresco dining. The room is large enough for a pair of chairs and small table in the corner – a pleasant sunroom sitting area.

The guest bedroom on the lower level features its own fireplace and seating area, letting guests retreat for private conversation without having to get right into bed.

Upstairs, working at home becomes a pleasure in a study that marries vaulted ceilings, exposed beams, and large windows with the furnishings of a corporate office, such as ambient wall lighting and an executive desk with visitors' chairs.

In the far wing, a luxurious master bedroom meant just for two is a dream come true for this family-oriented couple. A beautiful sandstone fireplace warms the room, from the sitting area before it to the canopy bed on the opposite wall. A private cedar deck lets the couple enjoy the view from their personal paradise.

Attached, the master suite features dual showers for convenient mornings, shielded by a curved room divider made of sparkling glass block. A single sink features vanity extensions to the left and right that provide his and hers counter space beneath twin windows.

Peaked Interest

Courtesy of MossCreek Designs

As if one could look right through it to the mountainous view beyond, this home of cedar peaks and skyward-reaching angles is like its own elegant mountain range. Layer after layer of variegated timber roofline keeps the eye guessing as it approaches the home down a brick driveway of tans and blues, arriving before twin entryways with stone and tree-trunk pillars. Throughout the home, combinations of stone, wood, and gray shingle contribute to an unmistakable mountain scheme that fits the setting and surroundings beautifully.

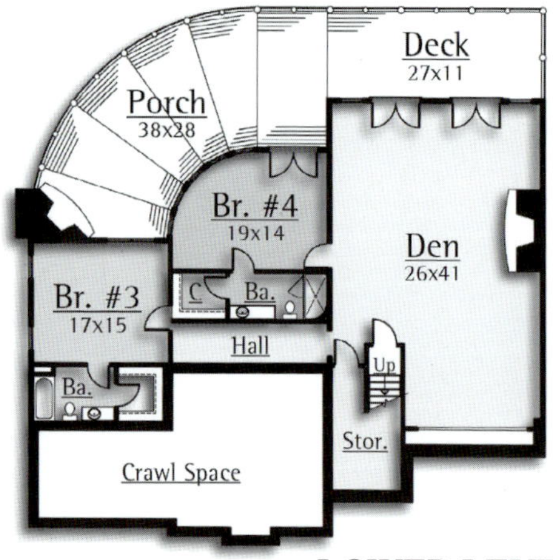

LOWER LEVEL

SECOND FLOOR

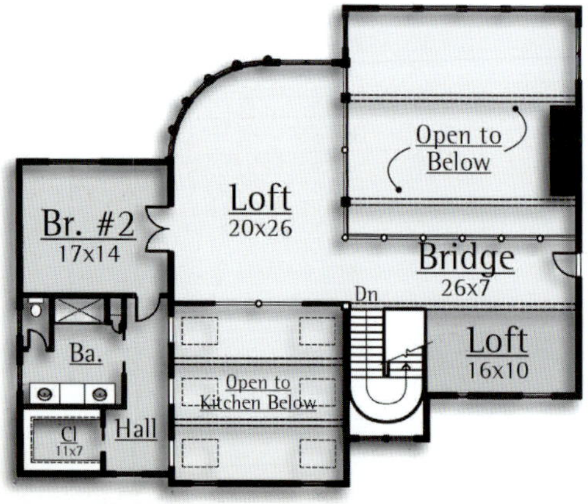

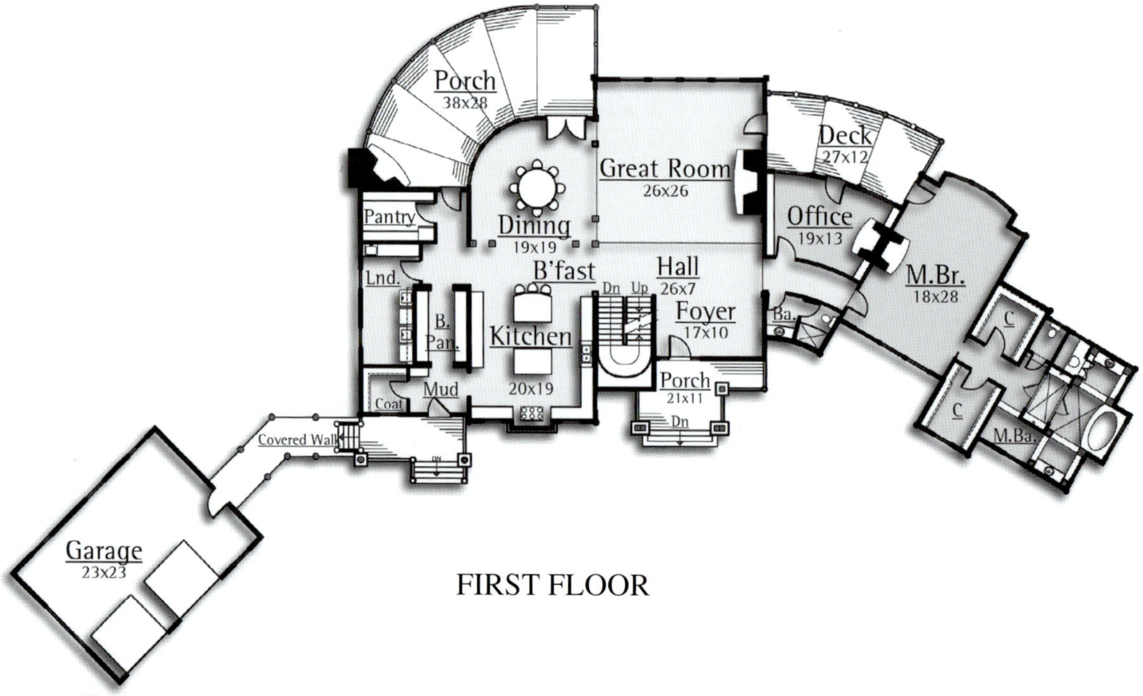

FIRST FLOOR

Classic Arts and Crafts Era twin entryways grace this home, the culmination of casual stone paths that lead to flagstone steps and ashlar pillars. Board and baton and rough hewn cedar siding combine with wood shingles and stacked stone for an artful introduction of the quality and artistry that lies within.

A stunning panorama of the home's front profile: a study of peaks and valleys. Across the driveway, a gentle brook flows between landscaped rock formations that echo the home's stone color palette. To the left, a three-car-garage with peaks of its own is connected to the house by a covered walkway.

On the main and lower levels, a covered porch features deep space for rain and sun shielded dining, reading, or fireside conversing. At the perimeter, tree like posts suspend the roof overhead, where dramatic timber framing reaches for the peak.

From this vantage point, the windows are omnipresent. They create a seamless flow between rooms, visually transporting us out onto the porches and into the wilderness.

The great room in this home feels uniquely warm and intimate for a room with such majestic soaring ceilings. On the far wall, a stacked stone fireplace reaches floor to ceiling, employing a signature keystone framed design. A towering antler chandelier suspends over the sitting area, where a velvety sofa draws deep burgundy overtones from the wood of the doors, mantles, and overhead loft railings.

Timber trusses support the cedar clad ceiling while, lofts, libraries, suspended catwalks and other unique spaces wait to be discovered, suspended over the great room just beyond detailed wrought-iron railings. Wherever possible, peaked ceilings and doorframes grace the rooms. On the far left of the catwalk, a peaked cutout with wrought-iron railing overlooks the kitchen.

The enormous kitchen is ready for all of the everyday traffic, with wide walking space between counter and island. Antiqued cabinetry sharply contrasts dark wood trims and bright red dishware accents. Candlelit chandeliers illuminate the space elegantly.

In the next room, a dining table takes center stage under recessed lighting for evenings, and beside a stunning panorama of tall windows overlooking the covered porch. An almond, antiqued hutch echoes the kitchen cabinetry, visible through a timber frame pass through between the two coordinating rooms.

This room features plenty of light and a magnificent view from glass doors that open to a covered porch. Inside, almond cedar paneling covers the walls, and pale stone forms a large hearth, both hues keeping the room feeling bright and open.

Just a doorway down the hall from the great room is a rather regal powder room for guests, featuring a mosaic tile inset where an elegant stone sink is ready for freshening up. A candle chandelier of wrought iron completes the very European look.

Across the hall and adjoined to the master bedroom, a stylish cedar paneled home office makes working at home a pleasure. A large window with a dramatic column frame provides an escape to the mountains whenever needed, and a pretty tiled fireplace with twin built-in bookshelves lends a library-like feeling to this studious space.

The adjoining master bathroom suite features a vaulted ceiling and marble floor. Long, thin windows with wooden Venetian blinds surround the pure white soaking tub, and a large vanity mirror gives the large room the appearance of even more luxurious space.

The master suite is a sight to see, beautifully framed in soaring timbers and anchored by a massive stone fireplace. The room is ready for cozy nights of reading by a crackling fire, and falling asleep warmed by lingering embers.

Pale Palace

In the evening, a reflection of royalty appears in a private lake as the palatial cedar home comes alive. Warm light streams from expansive windows in regal peaks and dormers, and what seems like miles of decking trace horizontal lines across the back, providing dozens of perches for readers, stargazers, or visiting guests to have a moment with magnificence. Sparing no luxury, this home fulfills every dream of its regular inhabitants, while hosting and entertaining friends and families with comfort and grace that rivals a fine resort.

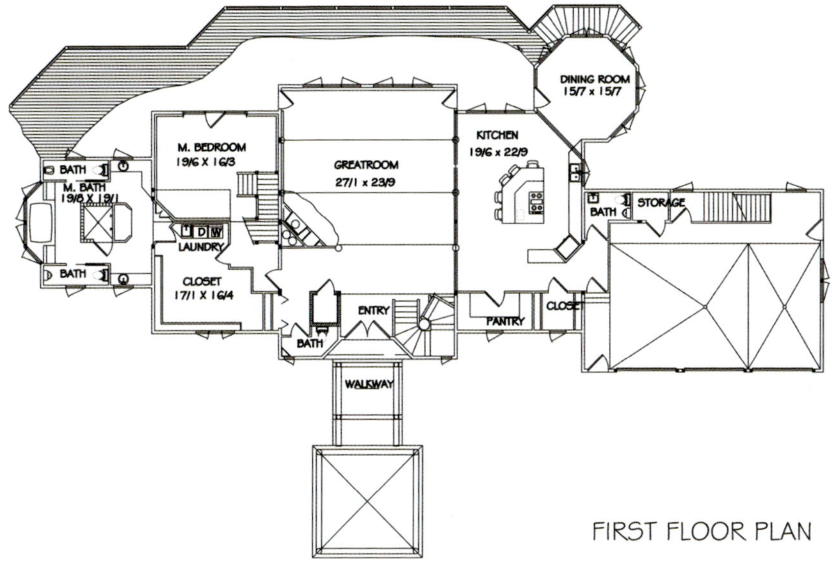

FIRST FLOOR PLAN

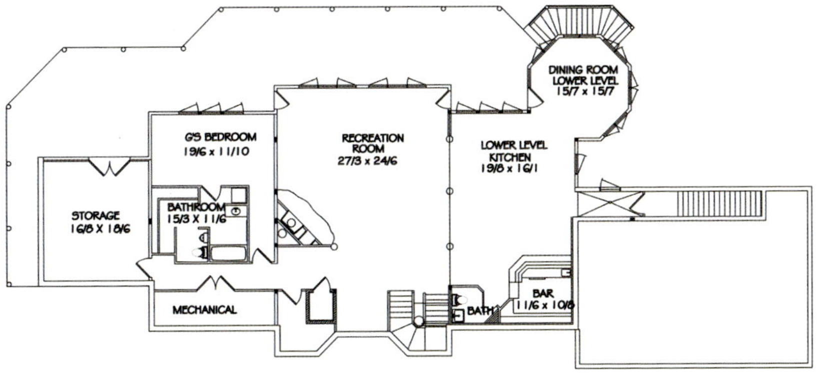

LOWER LEVEL PLAN

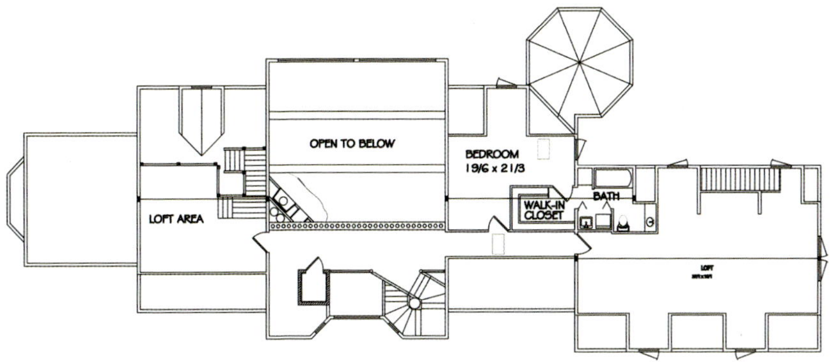

SECOND FLOOR PLAN

The front of the home is distinguished by a cedar porte cochére extending over the brick driveway. Visitors are led to the home's splendid front door and porch with a sense of anticipation and arrival.

Below the decks, the beautiful in-ground swimming pool trimmed with brick reflects the solidness of the fieldstone wall behind it, and remains neck and neck with the lake below for 'best place to swim' distinction.

Exploding with entertainment and sports opportunities, double deep decks ready with iron furnishings provide great dining, reading, lounging, and conversation spots. During inclement weather, a sunroom pulls its weight in providing unconditional access to the outdoors.

The kitchen repeats this dark-on-light concept successfully, with custom details that makes the space a chef's heaven. A concave bar creates a unique informal dining space that doesn't take up too much of the room. The kitchen prep area lies between the bar counter and the dining space, connecting the cook socially, and keeping food transfers from stovetop to table convenient. Beyond, a radial bay cedar dining area offers a 360-degree views.

Inside, soft, pale hues occupy the walls, ceilings, beams, and fireplace stone, allowing them to disappear as enclosures and leave the room feeling more open and beautiful. Dark carpeting and bold furnishings contrast exceptionally well, drawing out the deepest red and blue-gray river stones, knots in natural wood finished, and bright details such as the brass-trimmed hearth.

From this angle, note the functional and unobtrusive extra counter space that was wrapped around the wall from kitchen into dining space for useful, extra surface. A dark wood dining table and deep green tableware continue to offset pale structural details.

Downstairs, a second food and drink prep area is conveniently situated beside a large game and media room. Cedar vertical posts and paneling of light hues balance the light hues of flooring and furnishings.

Upstairs in the master bathroom, pale backdrops receive their darker treatments with green details in a pine motif that unites the walls, floors, tub enclosure, and window valance.

Next door, the master bedroom is served perhaps best of all by light hues that are naturally calming to the eye. A blue-green check pattern coordinates well with the cedar trim continued from the bathroom, and makes a refreshingly cheerful dust ruffle and curtain.

Split Personality

Each room in this splendid cedar home seems to have a personality of its own. With rustic, lodge like charms in some spaces, clean and contemporary lines in another, and oceanfront openness in still others, every mood is satisfied with a special space. Walking through the home, one is sure to find a room that was made just for them. Who says that you have to settle down in one place? Why not bring all of your favorite places to wherever you settle down?

Expansive pastures are marked by classic rail fencing.

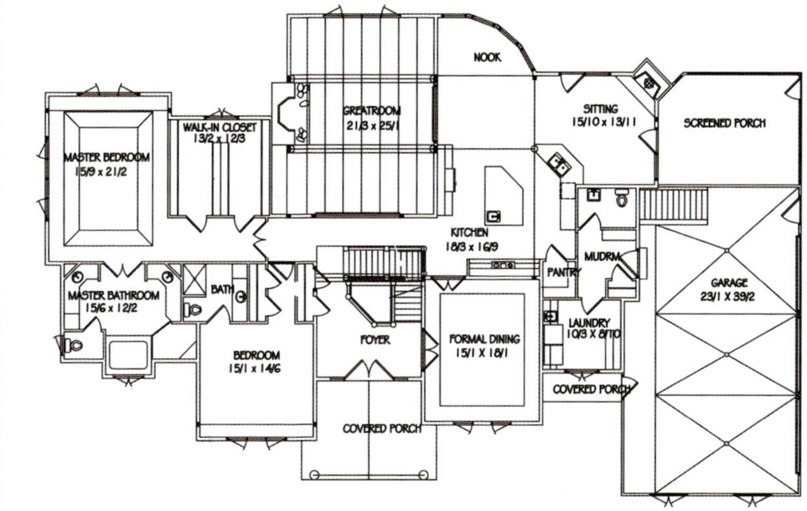

FIRST FLOOR PLAN

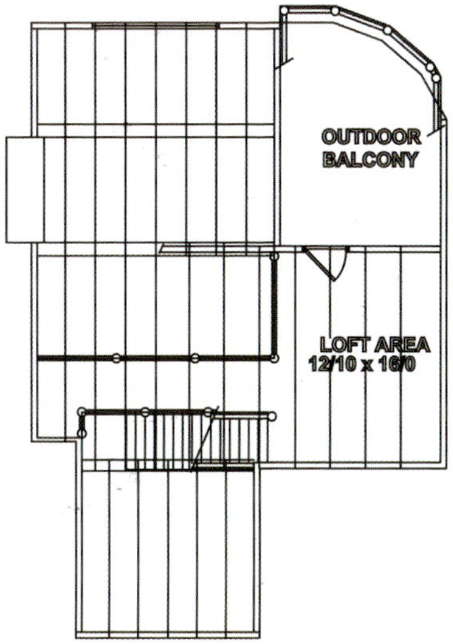

SECOND FLOOR PLAN

A carefully landscaped front lawn of red and green juniper beds leads to this natural cedar log home.

The back of the home features a brick patio ready with wooden benches for observing a spectacular view. River stone makes several appearances here for visual interest.

In the evening, the home emits a warm glow, illuminating an incredible hand-carved wooden door that recalls the Tree of Life's winding vines and roots.

As the front door's magnificent tree splits in two and its two etched glass panes open inward, a foyer of exceptional craftmanship emerges, with climbing staircases of natural log and massive exposed logs in wagon-wheel motifs overhead.

In the great room, giant log trusses oversee a cozy, cabin style living room of plaids and leathers, angled to face a pretty, splitstone hearth with natural log mantle. Chinking between the lodge log siding brings back the pioneering era.

A sunroom of beautiful floor to ceiling windows lends itself to an even greater feeling of outdoors with wicker furnishings and a slow moving ceiling fan that creates a breeze as natural as the real thing.

The dining room boasts a far more antiqued appeal with ornate wallpapered trim, high back chairs of carved wood designs, and a serpentine chandelier of deep blue green with candlewick lights.

In the kitchen, clean lines of white counters, stainless steel range hood, and angular cabinets keeps things feeling contemporary. Useful custom details like raised and extra outlets, bar-height counter, and built-in hutch speak of a commitment to functionality. A rustic atmosphere, however, pervades in the massive log and cedar paneled ceiling treatment.

A second, less formal eating area is perched inside a small, sunny outcropping – a modest breakfast nook with an incredible view.

Upstairs in the master suite, one feels as though they've walked right out of the mountains and onto a sunny beach. Pocketed lighting in a recessed ceiling keeps the lines of the room straight and clean; light fabrics and wicker furnishings recall an ocean front property's soft tones; tan hues underfoot result in subliminally sandy carpeting.